CRAZY ME

By Anna Maria Artist

Prologue

Read to me baby!... What can I say. My journey starts, I am ready to write this book. LOL (laugh out loud). I've never written a book before, in my home language or in English. But my publisher said it had to be written for all of those girls out there who's lives get screw by circumstances. Many short stories of my misfortune, happiness, horror, desires. I'll give you one example. I stole a baby when I was nine. Ha? And, what I have gone through will blow your mind and I'm pretty sure some of you may cry or disbelief. This book might be short but it is potent. So, buckle your seat belts and enjoy the ride.

Dedication

I dedicate this book to my living Angel. You will read about him as you follow my story. He remains nameless, but his compassion and generosity gave me the strength to continue. He showed me that the world is full of beautiful people. He knows who he is and how much gratitude I have for him.

Published in Melbourne Australia January 2025.

Heart Space Publications
PO Box 1085
Daylesford, Victoria, 3460, Australia
Tel +61 450260348

www.heartspacebooks.com
pat@heartspacebooks.com

All rights reserved under international copyright conventions. No part of this book may be reproduced, stored in a retrieval system, or transmitted in any form or by any means electronic, mechanical, photocopying, recorded or otherwise without written permission from Heartspace Publications.

Whilst every care has been taken to check the accuracy of the information in this book, the publisher cannot be held responsible for any errors, omissions, or originality.

Copyright: Anna Maria Artist

ISBN 978-1-7635657-2-2

Foreword

Life, a train carriage, clickity-clakking on a rail-line, going to who knows where. Hopefully the line travels to fulfilled potential, happiness, and prosperity.

Alas, events happen that are beyond our control, changing the direction, forcing the carriage to another line. Once redirected, the carriage trundles an uncertain course, without the ability to change track.

This line is long, dark, and full of derailments. Along the way rockfalls smash windows, bending steel. Extended tree branches scrape paint and bend the metal. At last, a junction offers a change of direction. Hope rises, perhaps sunshine? Less uphills?
It's not to be! The direction is different but the issues remain much as before. The carriage could give up or crash into oblivion. That is not its way – something keeps it going. An inner belief that things will be better.

As the years roll, although battered, our carriage does find a more comfortable track and happiness. Yet, it can never relax as it knows it is so easy to slip onto another track of uncertainty.

Anna's biography is like this train carriage.

Pat Grayson (author)

Contents

PART ONE – POLAND 11
- DADDY ISSUES 12
- Stop Please Daddy! 13
- Run away from home 16
- My baby! I found it! 17
- Golden goose or golden chicken? 19
- Confession 21
- Granny dearest 22
- Madhouse 23
- Knock knock 24
- Babysitter from hell 25
- Not again! Another Madhouse 26
- Parents day at school 27
- Curiosity killed the cat 28
- The mother I should had have 29

Part two – Australia 31
- The Nightmare 32
- School was fun. Not! 34
- Next-door neighbour 35
- Mother's lover 37
- Mummy dearest 38

PART THREE – THE WILD YEARS 41
- Bait 42
- Sex for the wrong reasons 43
- Popping my cherry 45
- Technology, lovely invention 49
- I have been to hell 50
- Passion for music 52

Prince charming...53
Filthy mistake..55
Exotic dancer..70
Can't touch this...71
NOW you're fucked!..72
Asian tour...72
Double Trouble – the twins..73
Fun club..74
Silent but deadly...75
Blow me..79
Safe speed limit..80
Let me pee...81
All for me?..82
21st century witch..84
Meeting my guardian angel...85
Golden years with my guardian Angel...86
Dangerous games...88
Stay away from my plate...89
Suit pants..91
Moment of truth...91
Don't judge...93
Meet Peter..93
Red flags...95
Again, My Angel to the rescue...96
Premonition..97
I see you mummy!...98
Honey I am back...99
Desperate to meet another angel..101
Run! Again run..104
Back to shit...105
Oh, Jackie boy...106

My stalkers...107
Breakdown..107
Honey I'm home..110
More jokes..112
Payback time..113
Never mind finding Memo! Finding dildo...115
My baby! 117
On the case..119

PART - FOUR Finishing up...121

I am an alcoholic..122
My Art...122
What makes me tick?..123
Mother..124
My Brother...124
Father...125
Spiritual beliefs – Gift or curse?..125
My Angel..131
Lee and Susanna...132
Their relationship with their father 134
Curiosity killed the cat 134
Dreams...136
Second chance..138

PART ONE – POLAND

1

DADDY ISSUES

I am a half breed of Russian and Polish blood, which explains my dark sense of humour. I was born in Poland, into a prosperous but dysfunctional family. The more money the crazier it became.

My father is a heavy alcoholic, but surprisingly active. It's just his mind that's screwed. Though he is cruel, I admire him. He drinks like a fish but still gets up early every morning to do a hard day's work. He must always build something. Never ending renovations. But that's him. That's his cover-up when he is depressed. He is street-smart, narcissistic, cruel, intelligent, strong, successful, artistic, and yet only a few see his other side...
But give him a bottle or two of vodka and the monster comes out. No woman is safe around him. He gets off on pain, inflicting pain to others, mentally, physically, or emotionally. He hates women.

His mother was cruel, to him, and later to me. His words, "Marry a young woman for a year or two, and then get yourself a new one! A younger version!" I didn't understand his arrogance, his hatred for women when I was listening to these grown-up conversations.

The house was always loud with music, and like all children, curiosity got the better of me. I would sneak quietly to the lounge room and listen to the 'grown-ups' talking. It was one time when I heard my father saying, "Women are only good for two things, fucking and cooking." I did not understand at the time what it meant as I was too young. But from his voice-tone I knew it was not good. I'm not keen to cook and only for my loved ones or for the occasional romantic dinner, as they say, "A man's heart is through his stomach."

When I was a young child, he used to scare the shit out of me. His athletic physique was strong, like a Russian bear. Mind you, he had two gold and a bronze medal for boxing as a middle weight.

PART ONE – POLAND

So, copping a punch from a man like that, as I often did, was terrifying. Especially a vulnerable, defenceless child. In a way, I'm thankful for my father for he made me a stronger woman because it was a case of: be weak and die or be strong and survive. Perhaps that explains why I'm a bitch. Well, if I'm a bitch, I'm a nice bitch.

As I said my father literally gets off inflicting pain on others. Unfortunately, I was often one of his victims. Just because I am a woman. The abuse! Verbal abuse, physical abuse, that I copped from him.

My brother did cop it but not as much as me. This is because he is a male, and I am a female.

Stop Please Daddy!

One day, I did something wrong. I can't remember what it was, but it was something little. This muscular man of 2.0m in height took his belt from his pants and was ready to hit me, until I bleed. I was hysterical and shivered in fear. I begged him not to hit me.

He stood holding the belt in the air, whilst laughing an insane laugh. He loved to see me grovel, whilst he held the power of life or death over me. With that laugh he said, "Come here, I won't hurt you". Then to trick me he would smile gently. Slowly, shaking like a leaf and full of tears, I crawled to him praying he would not strike me. When I was close enough, slowly he raised the belt, then with lightening speed struck me, hard. Then again, and again, all over my body. I covered my face with my hands and collapsed into the foetal position whilst he either hit with the belt, to the point of me bleeding, or punched me. And once he was done, and me like a beaten dog, he reached out his hand to help me up. And there he is the sweetest man in the world to help me recover from my wounds. I could call this a God complex. Or I could call it insane. I am not sure.

1

We used to go camping deep into the bush, always by a river. I liked camping, except when it came to swimming. I was scared to get into water, knowing that my father was watching and waiting for me. He would chase me into the deeper water and start drowning me. Literally, *drowning me*.

He would grab my head from behind by my hair and he would push me under the water and hold me there. After many seconds he would pull my head above the water and shout at me, "Do not scream! There is not enough time to catch your breath", and then he shoves me once again under water. I'm surprised I'm not afraid of water and I am a good, strong swimmer.

It's a love-hate relationship between us. Now, I understand his demons and the reasons for the way he is. It's an art to forgive someone. Especially when you were cut into a million pieces by the one you love.

One of his demons, that he *still* fights, is not trusting women. I can only surmise that it is because of his horrible mother. He has no respect for anyone, especially women. For God's sake, he married five or six times. I've lost count.

My father started without money, but as a florist the money flowed. The real wealth came when he extended his talents and his business into real estate. I learnt though, that money talks, bullshit walks.

He would tell me and remind me how stupid I am. I know I am not stupid; I am writing this for you, sharing my pain and experience but at the same time I want to show the world that if you put your mind to something you will get it. No matter how big the obstacle. Just believe in yourself and follow your instinct because it's there for a reason! As I say, "what mummy wants, mummy gets". Besides, he has his Karma, and I have mine. I feel and see remorse, and regret in him and that is dear to my heart. But he's still a prick!

PART ONE – POLAND

Because I'm a girl, he used to play serious mind games to the point that I thought I was crazy. Once, he paid money to a mental institute to have me locked in. This was in Poland.

My mother was his second wife. My brother (who shall remain nameless) and I are the only children he has – that we know of. When he married for the third time it was to a very cruel woman. She already had a son. He was older than me and had Autism, very intelligent as most autistic people are. When he was doing his Year eleven, he was so intelligent that he finished the year in six months and went straight to Year twelve.

My mother never cooked. We had nannies. And his various wives cooked but without interest. There were no happy family scenes of us sitting around a table, with a warm atmosphere. The food was uninspiring. And get this, if my father was to leave the table for any reason, he would spit into his food and say, "No one eats my food". There was no chance of that happening.

Children can be cruel because they do not understand the consequences of their actions. For example, I used to pick on my stepbrother, even though he was older. I would tease him because his motor skills and speech were wobbly. I'd imitate him in a nasty, cheeky way but he didn't mind. He was good to me and used to help me with my homework and other things. God bless his soul, and may he rest in peace as the poor bastard passed away in a car accident with his mother.

My father, brother, stepmother, and my stepbrother were in the car at the time. Fortunately, I was not with them. Guess where I was? In that mental Institute for children that my father put me in. I guess my dad having me locked in that placed saved my life. I get to those stories soon.

1

Run away from home

My stepmother was not kind to me or my brother. But the third lady my father wanted to marry (Ella) was a lovely, beautiful, kind and intelligent woman. She asked around about my father as to what kind of the man he was, before marrying him. His cruelty though was not known beyond the family walls, but it became apparent that he was not the right man for her and would not marry him. But to me and my brother she was gold. My heart was broken when she left my father. She was kind to me, warm hearted, artistic, and most of all, while she was with my father, she protected me and my brother from him.

Once, when I was about eleven years old, I had enough of the abuse from my father and his third wife. Yes, he got over Ella quickly and found himself a woman that did marry him. Anyway, I had saved the money from my communion and had about $5000. I took the money from the safe and I told my brother to put on his Boy Scout uniform as we were going to escape and go and live with Ella. Ella lived in another city, ten hours away.

We snuck out of the house and walked to the train station. We needed to buy a ticket for the trip but because we were so young I had to come up with a plan to buy the tickets without suspicion. I told my brother to go and stand next an old lady that was there and ask her for directions to toilet. At the same time, I went to the ticket counter and asked for the tickets.
The ticket-seller asked, "Where are your parents?"
I pointed with my finger to my brother and the old lady, telling her, "That's my grandma and my brother... I'm getting the tickets while they go to toilet". I waved my hand to my brother as a sign that I knew them. He returned the wave completing the sham.

The lady in the booth smiled and organised the tickets. I had to buy three tickets, so it looked real. A waste of money. But it was

PART ONE – POLAND

worth it for a moment knowing that we were on the way to our freedom.

The journey was long. When the time came for the conductor to check the tickets, he asked, "Where are your parents?"
I said to him, "We are with our grandmother, but she went to toilet. He punched the three tickets and went on his way".

When we got to Ella's city, I called her from a phone booth and told her that we are here. She was shocked and hurried to pick us up. She said she would have to phone our father and tell him we had arrived, otherwise he would be worried and was likely to call the police. My brother and I started crying, begging her to let us stay with her. Of course, we could not. We did not understand at that time why?

Because of the distance between our cities, Father only came the next day. And guess what happen? ... When we got home he gave me a belting. My brother did not cop it as much as me, because according to my father, whatever happened, it was always my fault. It was my idea. But even if it wasn't I would have copped it anyway.

My baby! I found it!

The event I'm about to relate would not even be seen in a movie. When I was about nine years old my mother sent me for milk. It was the very first time she sent me on my own. I clearly remember that day – a beautiful, sunny summer's day with a soft breeze. I walked via an alley, which was a shortcut to the shops. Within, there a pram stood between two buildings. I thought to myself, *where is everyone*? Looking around there was not a soul. Certainly, no parents. I looked into the pram. Mind you, the pram was my head height. I saw a child with a weird and strange cork in its mouth. I pulled out the cork, wondering why would someone

1

put a cork in a baby's mouth? Later I learnt it was a dummy. You see, in Poland the people are either poor or rich people with no class in between. The parents, obviously poor, made that dummy for the baby out of cork. They attach the rubber dummy sucker to the cork. Clever idea.

 Looking at the baby I was overwhelmed with all the things I did not have; love, trust, communication and most of all, safety. I felt for this child... I looked around. Still nobody, so I took the pram with me back home. Because I was small, pushing the pram was hard work. That did not stop me – the baby was mine and I was going to love it.

 When my mother saw me coming back with the pram, she almost had a heart attack, telling me that I must return the baby!
 I refused, "I found the baby! It's mine. It was abandoned between two buildings and there was no one there".
 Mother replied, "The mother probably placed the baby in the fresh air, whilst she watched from an apartment window. You must return that baby... NOW."

 I felt that I could never escape my life, it was too hard, there was nothing good in it. But this baby was good, and I would give it love. I was heartbroken, tears and snot ran down my face. I was a baby wanting to have a baby because at that time I always felt lonely and not loved. This baby would be mine and we would give each other unconditional love.

 I made my way back, struggling with that heavy pram. About halfway up the ally, a woman, a very frantic woman, was running towards me, waving her arms in anger, or fear, whilst screaming, "You stole my baby!! Why'd you take my baby?"

 As I got closer, I tried to explain to her that the baby was left on its own. But that have none of my pleas. She was yelling and screaming and other stuff, which I did not care to hear because I was too busy shitting my pants. All I could think off was owwww! My God! She's gonna kill me! Run!...

Now as a mother I understand her panic and anger as having a child stollen would be the worst nightmare for any parent. I bet she never left her child alone again.

Untouchable
An unborn baby in a full moon which represents the untouched soul of humankind that cannot be hurt or corrupted by life.

Golden goose or golden chicken?

We often went camping, especially in summer. Dad had a caravan, always the top brand, and brand-new. He looked after these very well. Of course, we had tents. Guess who slept in the tents? My brother and me...

I loved the camping... I still do, especially glamping. Anyway, we

1

would play inside the caravan during the day when we were not swimming. As a little girl I remember the fun of jumping from one posh seat to another. The material of the seats always smelt brand-new and clean, yet we were not allowed to sleep inside. Bloody prick…

We had everything with us, it was like paradise. All the food that you can eat, freshly made. Nice juices. I remember the smell of the meat on the BBQ.

On the occasion that I am about to talk about, I was about ten-years-old. It was a Sunday morning, a beautiful summer morning. The early sun shone on the grass and through the leaves of the trees. The freshness of the air and nature was gorgeous. But one problem, we had no eggs for breakfast.

Father told us go to the village and buy eggs and gave us 100 'Zloty' (Polish currency), which at that time would be equivalent to $15 in today's money – a lot of money just for eggs. Off my brother and I went to the village.

Most Polish people take religion seriously and as the church bells rang in the local village, the people left their houses and walked to the church. Because these are small villages, everyone knows everyone else so when they go to church they don't bother locking or even closing their doors.

With no one about we went to a house and found our way into the chicken coop. All the chooks squawking and so was quite scary. They were big motherfuckers. We scared the chooks out of the shed and into the chook-yard by flapping our arms and shouting. Looking around, I saw a nest full of eggs. I collected these and put them in my shopping bag. The eggs were still warm, which I guess was normal as we had just scared the chicken away that had been sitting on them.
In return for the eggs, we left the 100 Zloty in the nest.

When arriving back at the camp we told Father how we got the eggs. The first thing the bloody scrooge asked, "So you left the whole 100 Zloty there?".

"Yes", I said.

For moment he was quiet, then gave a strange smile and replied, "Somebody's going to have an interesting Sunday. Can you imagine when those people returned from church and finding 100 Zloty instead of eggs in the nest?"

As I said before that was a lot of money back then and those villagers were poor so I can just imagine their joy, and feeling very blessed. Maybe next time they prayed twice as much.

But when my father cracked open the eggs onto the frying pan, we had a big surprise – the eggs were too developed, and the chicks were almost fully formed. I guess it's safer going to the supermarket, so you get real eggs.

Confession

I was only about ten at the time and already every priest's worst nightmare... Every time at confession I would ask the priest for *his* confession. Or I asked them to explain the meaning of a woman and man being together. That used to embarrass the hell out of them or make them angry.

"Father, why aren't you allowed to get married?" "Oh father, but God created a woman and man to be together. Please explain? I'm asking you because you know everything."

They got the shits and shooed me out of confession box and told me not to come back. For some reason that satisfied me, seeing them frustrated and angry. I knew in my heart that most of them are not as pure as they say they are.

1

I did not want Communion, but religion and parents had the greater say. I didn't want to have my hair cut short, which was not necessary for a communion. Even though I was a tomboy, I wanted to look pretty with longer hair. I did not like all the girly-girly stuff. Nevertheless, I went and was a good girl for my mother and father or get belted.

These days it has no effect on me and I don't care one way or another. I did not force my girls to be communed and they chose not to.

Granny dearest

To my knowledge my father only has two children, and they were with my mother. He didn't have any children from a previous or subsequent marriage. But he sure had many lovers on the side. His nickname is Rooster. Come on people, use your imagination. What does a rooster do? He fucks all the chooks. Father could be charming when he wanted

Obviously, my father was brutalised by his own mother. She was a cruel woman, being mentally and verbally abusive as well being physically abusive.

She lived about three hours from us and every time we visited, no sooner I walked in, she would belt me with a tightly rolled-up tea towel. It felt like being whipped. One day I shouted at her, "Why are you hitting me?"
She said, "Before you do something wrong". She did not need a reason. She was just horrible. It was not just Granny that was nasty. On one occasion, it was winter, and I was wearing a bright red jacket. That jacket had some sort of weird effect on my grandmother's rooster. You cannot be hurt by rooster, right? Wrong!!! When I went out to the backyard where the rooster was, it jumped

me. I think I was eight years old and so this thing was half of my size. Not to mention how heavy it was.

This huge rooster became agitated and started pecking my head, over and over again. My parents and grandparents thought it hilarious as they watched from the window. Even though I was crying and getting hurt, it amused them. Finally, they came to rescue me when they saw my face covered in blood.

But that fucking rooster – who won, as later we ate him.

Madhouse

There was a time, one beautiful morning, I woke up to lovely music – Boney M. My father used to put music on early in the morning when he was in good mood. He loved Bony M. He loved music and he was a very good dancer. Anyway, I used to enjoy waking up on those days, because I knew there is no fighting between my parents.

On this morning, I woke up slowly, feeling calmer until I opened my eyes. Around me were about twenty other beds with children, and bars on the windows. It was then I remembered *I'm stuck in a mental institute*, one that my loving father put me in. All the young children around me appeared to me as aliens. I couldn't understand them as they had some sort of mental illness. I was only twelve at that time, and terrified that I would end up like them. And yet, why was that Bony M music playing? Till this day I do not know why. Did my father pay them to play this music on this particular day just to fuck with my mind? He kept me there for about a month and I made no friends. Staying with those loonies was so hard. The workers there were unfriendly and not nice. I was panicked and had to get out of there.

Unfortunately, in those asylums, the children were molested on

1

a regular basis. I am sure my father knew this. In this mental institute there was a gardener who was a child predator. I did not know that they existed but writing this as an adult I fully understand.

As a gardener he had a shed. This paedophile, who was about fifty, had an eye on me. He lured me to his shed. Being young I did not understand the danger and so I entered. It was dark, cold, and had no windows.

Somehow, I knew this was bad and ran out of the shed. My guardian Angel was watching my ass! I know that... But now I wonder how many little souls had been abused by that man in that shed, and not one of them would have been reported to management, even if the management cared.

I told nobody of this incident because I did not understand it. But it was the last straw, I had to get out. I climbed the fence and escaped and found my way into a village. Some people saw me and said they would call my father. I gave them the number and told him where I was.

Father arrived and his face looked on fire. But he could not show his anger to those nice people. I copped the belt and punches afterward. There was no point in me telling him what happen, he would only laugh and tell me that I am fucked-up in the head.

Knock knock

Our parents loved going to parties, where often they would leave us alone in the house. Sometimes we did have a nanny to look after us. But on this night we were left home alone. I was six, my brother was five. Of course, when parents are out children get up to no good. We wanted to get out of our room, but they locked us in. We just mucked around in the room, playing with toys, jumping on beds, and making noise – just the normal stuff.

PART ONE – POLAND

My brother pissed in my shoe because he could not get out to go to the toilet. That little bastard should have pissed in his own shoe, but no, it had to be mine. I was angry and started screaming at him. Suddenly, there was a knock on the door. To this day I am not sure if our father returned to scare us. We quickly jumped back into bed, got under the doona, and stayed quiet as a mouse. We were anxious and confused because we knew there was no one in the house, but who knocked on the door to our room? I have this suspicion that he came back from the party to check on us. And why not play a practical joke by knocking on the door to scare the shit out of your children. Sadistic bastard.

Babysitter from hell

Sometimes we had a babysitter come and look after us. Or from time to time, we went to her place where a few other children were being looked after. Here was another vicious old hag. My father loved her, not in a romantic away, but because she was malicious.

If I answered her back, she would go to the garden and pick a nettle. These had tiny spikes on the leaves. To the naked eye you could not see the prickles. She would grab me by the hair and rub the leaf across my face. It stung like crazy, and my face would swell up to the point that I could not see nor breathe.

To her any excuse to be cruel to us was enough, naughty, or well-behaved, it did not matter. Once it was so bad they had to take me to emergency.

When the time came for an afternoon nap, she would show us a book with vicious looking crocodiles (to children, all crocodiles look vicious). She would say, "If you don't sleep this crocodile will come and bite your feet off" and take glee in telling us stories of children being eaten by crocodiles.

1

How could we sleep? We were terrified. Then when we tried to settle, that sadist would crawl along the floor to make us think it was a crocodile coming to eat us.

A bitch for a child minder and a prick for a father, nice combination two psychopaths.

Not again! Another Madhouse

After I ran away from the first madhouse that my father had me locked in, he decided to lock me up in another but further away from our city and in the bush. He reckoned if I ran away, I would get lost in the bush.

This madhouse was an old castle. Lots of secret rooms, chambers, and passages to get out of the castle or get into the basement. That was the time my father's wife, the one with the autistic son who died in the car accident. My stepmother was driving when they crashed with a bus and the car rolled over three times. My stepmother and stepbrother died immediately. When the rescue crew pulled my father out of the car a shoe dropped out. As the officer picked up the shoe he realised there was another body under the car – this was my brother who they saved.

And was my father hurt? No. Just a broken jaw. After that accident my father's brother and his wife, my auntie, arrived at the madhouse to pick me up and leave that horrible place behind. I believe in my heart that if that accident did not happen, I probably would be still in that madhouse or worse.

PART ONE – POLAND

Queen of the damned
A beautiful Queen, charming and desirable. She has her wick ways of possessing anyone or anything she wants, but yet, the only one thing she desires she cannot have. True love. To be loved for herself not her beauty or for what she can do. She is trapped in her own prison, therefore no one can see her true heart and her good intentions.

Parents day at school

In my Polish school, each student had a report card, reporting on behaviour, subject marks, and all the rest. When it was time to give it to my parents to examine and to sign, I was anxious beyond belief as I knew that when my father read it, I would get another beating. No matter how well I did, my father would find fault with me. I was terrified and signed it for him, so the teachers would leave me alone. They knew that my father was strict, but they did not know how cruel he could be behind closed doors. Of course, he would find out sooner or later when the meeting with teachers came around.

Curiosity killed the cat

One day, my second stepmother sent me to the shops. When I returned the door was locked. I banged on the door to be let me in. Frustrated when no one opened the door I went around the back of the house where my parent's bedroom was and looked through the window. I'm about to knock on the window when I saw my father getting down to business between my stepmother's legs. I was horrified, not understanding what was happening. As is natural I was curious – why did my stepmother let my father do such a thing. I could not ask my father because I knew I would get belted, plus it was embarrassing. What do I do? Perhaps I should ask my stepmother. As she is a woman to explain it to me. When I asked her what my father was doing between her legs, she went red. She would not give me an answer and changed the subject. But later, she told my father, and as usual he beat me with the belt. I was angry and confused. Why would she tell him what I asked her? I thought that by asking her it would just be between us girls. How wrong was I. That bitch! From that day I never asked her anything personal.

When I was a young Polish student I was not a good student. I had little interest, was bored, and pissed off with life, so I hardly paid attention. I did not learn as much as I should have.

Nor did my Polish teachers like me – I was strong-headed and opinionated. She did not like that. Some teachers should not be teachers, and in some cases, teachers can learn from us – meaning the children.

Once at the end of the school year she asked the class to come to her place to help her clean. For that we would get extra credits. The next day I arrived at her house but no one else showed up. She was surprised that out of all her students I was the only one. She was amazed as she considered me a lost cause, just a naughty kid with no future.

Actually, we had a nice day, where we got to know each other. I helped her wash the windows and vacuumed.
The next day she embarrassed the shit out of me. In front of the whole class, she announced how proud and grateful she was to me as I was the only one that came.
I used to sit at the back of the class, trying to be invisible, and here she was raving on about how well I did. I was an odd kid without many friends. Anyway, I guess she learnt a lesson that day – don't judge a book by its cover.

The mother I should had have

From time to time I would sneak out to see our next-door neighbour, Mrs. Polsky. She had two teenage sons but always wanted a daughter. I did not have much to do with the sons, and they wanted nothing to do with me. I always wanted a mum to be close to me. I suppose we both filled in the holes in our hearts when we were together. She was kind to me, soft and gently spoken with a big heart. When I visited she would make me a beautiful soup made from cherries. When we finish eating we would usually go to her garden and do some gardening, which I loved doing with her. Sometimes, late afternoons we would both snuggle up in her bed and watch TV. She would let me eat in her bed while we watched a movie. Her husband was uncomfortable with this and would get out of bed and go to the lounge room. But Mrs. Polsky and I had the time of our lives.

Mrs. Polsky was always there for me. Every time my parents

fought, I would sneak off to her place because I knew I would have peace and quiet there. Instead of punches, I'll get hugs.

Part two – Australia

2

The Nightmare

When my father didn't drink, he was a fabulous man. Wise, kind, and understanding. OMG! Who am I kidding!... The man was a ruthless bastard. But yet, he holds such knowledge. What a waste.

When I was a child I had a recurring nightmare. It was always the same. In the dream I wanted to fly away. To do so, I just flapped my arms and I would fly. But each time I had the dream I would fly close to electrical power lines that connected house to house. The closer I got to them, the more they closed in on me. I was afraid of electrocution. Yet, I was powerless to fly away from them.

All changed after I arrived in Australia. I had that same dream/nightmare one last time. This time when I neared the electrical lines they moved out of my way. I was free. I was finally free of my father's mental and physical abuse. He could not touch or scare me anymore. He was too far away. What a relief.... I felt a stronger love for him when he was far away... I was also relieved as I thought I had moved away from all the sexual predators, so I thought.

You may be wondering how come my controlling father let me escape his control by letting me move to Australia. It had to do with my behaviour. I wanted to be with my mother and so constantly played up. I was too much of a hand full to him and he was getting tired of me. Then, when my mother offered to pay for the ticket he jumped at the chance. Thinking about this as an adult, I think he would have thought, *you beauty, let me get rid of her*. For me to get away from his brutality and go to my mother was the best of two evils. My mother showed little interest in us but at least I was not going to be beaten.

When I was young I don't remember playing with dolls but I

Part two – Australia

had a big stuffed monkey that was orange. I never went anywhere without that monkey. I called it Malpa (monkey in Polish). When I was leaving Poland for Australia my father would not let me take Malpa. His excuse, that the monkey will get torn apart at the airport when they do inspections. I didn't want Malpa to be ripped apart, so I left him behind.

My father wanted to fuck with my head, for this last time, showing the power he had over me, right to the last second.

He put me on the plane on my own. My brother only came two years later when our mother could afford the extra ticket. My father asked some strangers (other passengers) to keep an eye on me until I landed in Sydney Australia. I was so scared I had nowhere to run. Well, in that situation only a moron would trust total strangers to look after a young girl. And yes, that would be my father, a moron and brilliant at the same time. And I just turned fourteen years old.

I was stuck on that aeroplane, without company or support, on my way to an unknown place called Australia. But at the same time, it was exciting as it was my first time on a plane. But holy shit, it was a long way from Poland to Australia. We had to change planes in Singapore and from there we flew to Australia.

I arrived in Australia on 25th April in 1990. I was excited that I would get and to see my biological mother, who came here two years earlier.

Before she left, she couldn't tell us that she was leaving for Australia because, Control Freak Father would have tried to stop her. He would pay whoever he needed to make sure that she could not leave. Just! Because he can...

I was so happy to see Mum at the airport, and in that moment I forgot all the pain, the fear, the loneliness, and fear of my father's beatings and his emotional torture. It was only later that I realised why she wanted me – to look after her as a live-in servant. And, of

33

course, it was the same old stuff where she was never there for me as you will see as you read on.

*Trapped soul.
Represents struggle of life. Struggle between the inner self of good and bad.*

School was fun. Not!

I was eager to learn English and needed to understand what people were saying to me. My mother signed me up to school ASAP as I had no knowledge of English speaking, reading, or writing.

Of course, I was bullied at school because I was not born here – an outcast. I could not make friends because I could not speak English. I didn't even finish year nine. It was difficult because everyone interacted in English, and I was the stupid alien. I quit school without English writing or spelling.

Part two — Australia

Next-door neighbour

We lived in an apartment block, and I was lucky to have met Laura, who lived next door and went to the same high school. We became friends. I used to go to Laura's place to visit her and her younger siblings. There was a swimming pool in the complex and we all played together when the weather was nice.

Laurie's parents were always around, keeping an eye on us. The mother was a nice lady. She was kind, cheery, and treated me like I was one of her own. Lauren's father was quiet, but I often noticed him watching me.

One day I went to Lauren's apartment to return a video I had borrowed. Bob, the father, opened the door. All he had on was a towel around his waist. He invited me in and closed the door behind me and stood against the door. I felt uncomfortable because the house was not its noisy self. I asked him if the children were around.

"They unexpectedly went overseas for a holiday with my wife. They'll be back in two weeks." The way he looked at me gave me the creeps. I tried to distract him. Looking around the apartment I saw a guitar. Trying to change the atmosphere and somehow get out of there, I asked him, "Do you play the guitar?"

He nodded, still looking at me.

I asked him if he would play something.

He said, "Better yet, I can show you how to play" and told me to sit on the couch. This was a bad idea. He grabbed the guitar and settled next to, and slightly behind me, and with determination placed his arms around me to show me how to hold the guitar.

As he snuggled closer, I knew I was in trouble and struggled to get up off the couch. He quickly pushed me to the floor and threw himself on top of me, put his hands under my dress and tried to remove my panties. I started crying and begged him to let me go. The more I begged and cried the more aroused he became.

2

We lived in an apartment block and if I screamed the whole building would hear me. So I shouted to him, "If you don't let me go, I'll scream." He immediately rolled off me. I, like a released rabbit, shot out of that apartment in no time.

I told no one about this as I was embarrassed, and ashamed. When his wife and children returned, with them was a teenager girl, apparently from her previous marriage. That is why they went overseas, to get this daughter. Mary was two years older than me, and at sixteen she was tall and athletic. Quite intimidating, compared to my 'little-girl' body of that time.

She quickly made friends with other students at school. One of them was a dwarf. And the reason why I mention this is because this little dwarf bullied me, pulled my hair, scratched and hit me. I called this bunch 'The Mean Bitches'.

Because of what happened with Laura's father I had no idea what he would tell them, if anything?... And I was too young and naive to understand the conniving games of grown-ups. I was soon to learn.

From that time onwards, those 'mean girls' started a hate campaign against me. For months I copped physical abuse, verbal abuse and emotional abuse from Mary and her friends, including that bloody dwarf.

When I walked to school, they stalked me. They threw stones at me, called me horrible nasty names, "Whore. You try to fuck my father... Slut." They pushed me around, punched me, pulled my hair.

I was on my own and scared. Their violence did not stop at school. They were even in front of my house at night, throwing rocks and raw eggs at our windows, screaming, "Slut, whore. You try to fuck my father!!"

I was constantly in fear and didn't even feel safe at home. My mother wasn't much of a help as she just ignored it all. Finally, she was tired of the ruckus and told me, "Go to the police and report the man."

I asked, Okay, when are we going?

"You go on your own."

Great, I was fourteen and had to go to the police station and lay a rape charge on my own. Thanks Mom.

Hardly speaking English, in a strange country, terrified and not knowing Australian law I went to the local police station. But I did it! They listened and filled out the forms.

The case went to the court, and he (the prick) tried to say it was my fault. The judge did not believe that a young, fourteen-year-old girl virgin would try to rape a middle-aged man. Bob was found guilty of attempted rape and deported. Whoopee!

My mother did not go to court with me and pretty much ignored all that went on and how it affected me over the months, because of the abuse that I took from those Bitches, the attempted rape, the court case, and deportation. As long as there was peace in the house, she didn't give a damn how I felt or how much I needed her at that time.

That was rape attempt number two.

Mother's lover

At that time, my mother worked for some big company. She also was the mistress to a married guy. Later, fortunately, he passed away. Yes, you read that right. The guy was a prick.

One day I was sick and so did not go to school. Mother was at work during the day from 9:00 AM to 6:00 PM. I did what every child does when sick, which was to go to Mum's room and climb into her bed. It's a security blanket. And even now, my children at nearly twenty, come and lay in my bed when upset, sick or overly tired.

This boyfriend had the keys to our house and could come in anytime he wanted. My mother was devoted to him one hundred percent. All about Mario! This day, around 3:00PM he came and let himself in. This was just before school finished. He walked into my mother's bedroom where I was sleeping. Seeing me, he got into the bed and tried to spoon me. I jumped out of the bed and ran into my room and locked myself in. I could hear him stomp past my bedroom door several times, and then heard the main door slam as he left the house.

I did not know what to say to my mum about this. It took me a week, before I had the courage to tell her. Typically, she had excuses for him, "Oh... he probably thought you were me". Bullshit!

A week later I tried again. This time her reaction was different, saying that I was the guilty one. That I tried to get to into the bed when he was sleeping." Seriously?! What the fuck...

At the time her hair was blonde, I am brunette. I could not believe that she would make those suggestions.

Mummy dearest

Once again, my mother was not there for me. But when it came to parties, going to clubs and the like, she was the first to arrive. Like the Queen as she entered the building. She always made sure to tell me, "I never wanted to have children", and she was saying that shit to me!...

When she told me these things it was always with resentment,

Part two — Australia

as if to make me feel guilty. I asked her, "Why tell me that? I'm your daughter and it hurts". She would fall silent and not say anything — the damage done.

When she was with my father, there were always parties, or big events. She even had her own tailor to custom make her dresses. My communion dress was done by her tailor. But that design was mine. I remember my mother and the lady sitting together at the table, discussing what dress to make for my communion (this was still in Poland). I was with them, and silently grabbed paper and pen and designed a dress in less than five minutes.

My mother and the lady looked at each other in surprise. And, I am pretty sure that was the only moment that my mother ever felt proud of me. As a mother should. I did not think anything of it, as to me it was no big deal.

Soon after that Mario issue, and with the next-door neighbour event my mother kicked me out. I had to go and live on the street, or anywhere, "Just get out". Here I was in a strange country, with very little English, I just turned fifteen, and she kicked me out. I was scared and confused. Where was I to go, how could I survive?

PART THREE – THE WILD YEARS

3

Bait

One day, before I was kicked out, Mum and I went to visit an auntie. She lived ten minutes away from the beach. When we arrived, she was happy to see us and had made a beautiful meal for us – everything was going to be great, and later we were to go to the beach.

At that time, I did not know about marijuana or its aroma. Aunt and Mum had a joint. Their behaviour became obnoxious where they started behaving like clowns towards me, with hysterical laughter. I could not understand this weird and insulting behaviour so decided to go to the beach on my own.

The water was great until…. Well, I was wearing a G-string bikini and of course I was stung on my ass by a bluebottle. And that bitch hurt like hell.

Being angry with my mum and auntie I didn't bother calling them to pick me up. Besides, I didn't think they were capable of driving, so I started walking to my aunt's. Then a guy pulls over next to me in his convertible. A beautiful red sports car. He notices I was in distress and asks. "You okay?"
"No! I'm not."
"Do you want lift home"
I hesitate because I didn't know him. But it was a nice car… and I was hurt, the weather was hot, and I did not want to walk so far in the heat.

Fuck it! I thought, why not. He doesn't look like a serial killer but who knows what they look like? Climbing into the car I said I don't want to go home yet.
He replied, "We can go to my friend's house for a while. He has a nice swimming pool."

I learnt that the driver's name was Sam and Sam's friend's name

PART THREE – THE WILD YEARS

was... well I would just call him Shithead. They were both about thirty years old, I was nearly fifteen, and green.

He had a beautiful big pool, so we swam for a while. Shithead was a smooth talker, filling me with all sorts of lies. We had sex. I only had sex with shithead, not Sam. He did not take my virginity, I will get to that later.

When he had finished, I asked him, "What's now? Are we going out to dinner?" I was scared and confused, not knowing what would happen between me and this guy. Shithead.
"Sure, I'll take you out for a romantic dinner. But don't you think you need to get back home?"
At first, I didn't understand that he wanted to get rid of me as soon as possible after he had his sex. Once he dropped me off at my aunt's house, I realised he did not give me his number.

After all that shit going on between my auntie and my mother, and on top of being played and used by that man I felt more anger, frustration, sadness, emotionally and physically abused. I had been used, just a piece of meat, shamed, and felt disgusted.

At my auntie's place they were still behaving like idiots. I had enough so I went back to my mother's home on my own, where I locked myself in my room and cried, clutching the pillow to comfort me.

Sex for the wrong reasons

Many men tried to rape me, and some succeeded. I choose to not include all these stories. Not because I am ashamed or embarrassed, it's because I don't want you to see me as this poor girl. Rather see me as a survivor, one that fights every day, whilst retaining a wicked sense of humour, despite my Demons.

3

You think at the young age (as a teenager) that you know it all! How gullible we are at that age. My daughters are my biggest triggers for bringing me back to my teenage years. How naive, innocent, gullible and pure of heart. If you are a parent reading this book, my advice, which you can take or leave – and I mean it with respect to you – when you have a problem with your obnoxious, out of control teenagers, that you want to just kick their ass to knock some sense into them, remember, you were once that young too, and remember what was going through your mind at that time. Were you afraid? Emotionally frustrated, hurt, not seen or even just sexually frustrated. Well, for men, poor guys with all that sperm count, mounting daily how the fuck can they concentrate on other things when the mind is constantly thinking of sex. I mean poor boys and girls.

Young girls have sex, mostly for the wrong reasons. Often they are hang overs of 'daddy issues' – where the father relationship was not a healthy relationship, like for example: an alcoholic, user, workaholic never home, emotionally unavailable, liar or even a cheater. There could be lots of reasons that can lead young girls having sexual relationships, just to feel loved by men. Unfortunately, those men are dirty players there take advantage, telling young girls what they want to hear, and then he's gone once he had the sex. The girl is left feeling abused, hurt, used and ashamed.

But some girls do it just because they have a high libido. Those girls are usually called sluts. Why it is okay for men to have a strong libido without calling them names? Yes, a woman is a slut. Double standards! My advice to you lovely young people, always follow your gut feeling, because it is there for a reason. If you feel something wrong is about to happen, don't do it! I tell my girls to listen to your heart but follow your brain.

And then you have the Casanova! There is a big difference between a dirty player and a Casanova. A Casanova makes you feel that you are the only woman for him. He offers you respectful words. He takes his time to get to know you and pretends that he will not leave you feeling like you have been used. And a Casanova comes back to the same woman, for a while. Therefore, you don't feel like you've been used. And Casanova has lots of lovers at the same time, which he treats with respect. And even so, he makes the woman or girl feel like she's the only one for him in that moment. And Casanova adores all woman.

Then you have predators that just pray on the young innocent mind. They have no morals, no shame, no regrets, just the devious mind that would lead them to say or do horrible things to a young woman.

By listening to your heart but following your brain, believe me, you will save yourself lots of headaches and heartbreaks.

Popping my cherry

I came to Australia a virgin, despite having been sexually abused as a child. I was lucky or should I say, God blessed me and so my predators did not penetrate me.

I just turned fourteen years old when I arrived in Australia. So, you could say I was a fresh puppy. Sex was not on my mind. Nor was I interested in boys or girls. Quite the opposite, I hated men for a long time and did not want to be touched by them or have anything to do with them.

I used to have horrible nightmares, and all regarding men. For many years I had counselling, which did help a bit. But still, to this day when it comes to sex, I have difficulties engaging in it. With the thought he is just using me for my body.

With my weird sense of humour, I turn sex to jokes. That's how I deal with my Demon. But people take me the wrong way. They think I am a sex maniac or dying for a fuck. But my friends, the ones who know me well, know that my sexual jokes are just a cover to protect myself from my trauma.

Some people call my jokes flirting, but really, I'm just being cheeky and stirring shit. Unfortunately, men take this the wrong way until they get to know me. If they have the chance! When I flirt or am a bit cheeky, and if I notice that a man is attracted to me and wants more, I run the other way.

I know we live in this stupid society when it comes to men and women, where, if a woman chases a man or tries to get his attention, men get turned off. They think that the woman must be a slut. Not necessarily. But if a woman chases a man... The man runs the other way thinking the worst of her.

When I went to year nine at high school there was a boy (Jimmy) in year twelve. Jimmy was a few years older than me. He was the first male that I was interested in and so I observed him from a distance. I liked what I saw – he was athletic, tall, a bit shy, funny, charming when he wanted to be, and he was down to earth.

One day we locked eyes on each other. I had butterflies in my stomach because I was attracted to him. I didn't know at that time that he liked me as well. I asked my girlfriend Nikki if she would introduce us.

She did, and from the start we hung around together. I communicated with my broken English, but he understood me. He was patient and kind to me. He didn't indicate or make any suggestions about sex with me. Because if that was the case, I would have run a mile.

Jimmy started coming over to my house, we played games on the computer, or we would go to the park to make out. Just kissing, a nothing else. Over the time though, as we became closer, we became sexually attracted to each other. I told him I was a virgin, and I would like to lose my virginity with him. He asked me my age,

PART THREE – THE WILD YEARS

"nearly fifteen", I told him. His response was, "No, we should wait until you're fifteen". My heart skipped a beat and I gained even more respect for him by the way he respected me. But my desire for him sexually increased. I did not want to wait until I was fifteen. I wanted it then so badly. Still, we only mucked around with kissing, a bit of foreplay, and exploring our bodies with soft touch.

A few days later I told Jimmy, straight, "I'm ready… I'm not gonna wait any longer until I'm fifteen." His face turned red – I don't know if he got embarrassed or flattered by my determination. We set the day for the following Monday, where he would come to my place as my mother would be working late.

We were in my bedroom and started making out. His background was Vietnamese, and usually Asian men have small penises. But Jimmy had a huge one. That scared me. But he was not the one pushing for sex. He was patient and understanding. I wanted him even more.

The first time when he tried to penetrate me, I panicked and asked him to stop. He respected my wishes and backed off. I asked him if we could try again, tomorrow, and not to go to school? He agreed to come back to my place the next day. As usual, a little foreplay, kissing, and we tried again. As he started to enter me, only a quarter of the way in, I was in pain. Again, I asked him to stop and try another time. Jimmy was so patient and agreed to leave it for another day. On our third attempt we went all the way. Losing my virginity hurt like a bitch. But he was slow and gentle.

There are many young boys who disrespect girls after getting what they want but Jimmy was different. He didn't give a damn what they said at school about us, and he didn't let anyone bully me after that.

As I mentioned earlier, my school days were horrible but with Jimmy on my side, it was easier. At the end of the school year, Jimmy finished his year twelve. The school wanted me to repeat

3

year nine, because I missed one hundred and fifty days and was so far behind. But I didn't want to go through year nine again so I left school thinking I will make my own way in my life. Jimmy and I kept in contact for a while but then we went our separate ways.

That's how I lost my virginity. Now, being older, I wonder was Jimmy a Casanova and knew how to get me from the beginning? Even if he was, that's okay because Casanovas love and adore woman and he was good to me. And let's not forget how charming he was! Farewell my Jimmy boy. Thank you for popping my cherry. LOL

And what did I feel once it was over?
After losing my virginity, I thought of myself like a woman, thinking that; *now I'm not a virgin I can conquer the world* – bullshit... It hurt like crazy. Nor was it like you see in the movies, full of passion and pleasure. It took us three times to go all the way. Although Jimmy was patient and gentle, I could not see the big deal as people make it up to be. I felt weird, and at the same time numb. It was as if I was not there mentally, just physically. But after a while, having regular sex with Jimmy it got easier. Yet, the feeling I had after sex; it was like a handshake, without emotion. I tried to deceive myself that I enjoyed it. The reality though, I did not enjoy having sex. Don't get me wrong, I would not change a thing about how I lost my virginity and have no regrets. I picked the right boy to pop my cherry. And, if you ask me, it is up to you girls, when you are ready you will know in your heart and follow your brain when the time is right.

Naïvely I did not think about getting pregnant. And lucky for me I didn't because I probably would have kept it just to be loved by someone. That would have been the wrong reason to have a child – it would be selfish of me.

Now, thinking about my foolish ignorance, having a child as young as I was would have complicated my life, more. I don't know

PART THREE – THE WILD YEARS

if I would have been responsible enough for all that it would have entailed – to care for a new life that would have been in my hands. I did not really know how to take care of myself, let alone a baby. And, being in this strange and new country, with little English, not knowing the rules or the law, nor having any support from parents or loved ones, it would have been very hard. Maybe, after a time, I would have started to hate the child. Yet, I always promised myself that when I was to have a child that I would do everything opposite to my parents. Give them love, affection, and most of all, to be there for them without fear. That my children would not be afraid of me if they want to tell me something. Now I am a mother, with grown up children, who are very close to me, my best friends, and they feel the same way about me. Yes sure… we have our moments, but I would not change it for the world.

Technology, lovely invention

It's hard to be a woman, single mother, even in this age. This is made harder when their English is not the best. Yes, I can speak well enough, well almost well. But to be honest my reading and writing of English is poor. How hilarious is that, that I am writing this book now?

Truth is, I hate new technology. It causes a lot of trauma and drama. But there is a benefit, 'voice recognition'. It cost me a lot of money but it's worth it as I just talk to it, and it immediately translates into text on the page. There are many funny things because of my accent, I confuse it. For instance, when I said drama above, it came onto the page as 'drummer'. So, what the hell, write a book. Whoops! Totally off topic.

3
I have been to hell

After my mother kicked me out, I felt alone because I was alone. I felt emptiness, pain, and fear. Before I left, I stole a hundred dollars from her purse. At least I had some money for food. But instead of food, I went to the doctors to get a prescription for sleeping pills. I could not bear any more pain, fear, or loneliness. I went to a park, sat down under a tree, and took all the sleeping pills. Now I can rest in peace, I thought to myself.

I have no idea who called the ambulance, but I ended up in hospital. At one stage I briefly woke up while I was transported to a hospital bed. I felt some creep touching my breast. I struggled to open my eyes to see who was feeling me. I could see a male figure above me looking down at me and touching my breast at the same time. I blacked out again.

Later, I woke up and all was dark. Above me, behind me, in front of me, all around me was black. I start walking not knowing where I was or where I was going. I could not find a light in the darkness. I called for help. There was no one there. It felt like I was travelling on foot for days, in this darkness, without human contact or anything familiar. It was real, until I finally I opened my eyes and found myself in a hospital bed, with drips attached to me. I was exhausted and annoyed, *Why I am still alive?* When I ripped the drip lines out of my veins the machine started beeping, loudly. A nurse rushed in.

I shouted to her, "Why am I still here?" She replied in a firm voice, "Calm down. If you won't be good, you'll go to the mental health unit".
Hearing those words brought back the horrible memories from Poland. I shut up. I was not giving any shit to that nurse.

I asked her, "How long have I been here?"

PART THREE – THE WILD YEARS

"You've been in a coma for five days".
Five days! *How was I in the coma when I was awake and stuck in that darkness?*
I asked the nurse, "Does my mother know I am here?"
"Yes, she does"
"Did she come to see me?"
"No".
"Is she coming to see me?"
"I don't think so".

I was depressed, even more. Especially knowing that my mother knew where I am, what happened to me, but doesn't give a damn. What a hard bitch I thought. *Screw her! It's my life! I'll not give her the satisfaction of needing her.*

After being released I did the rounds of staying with friends from school and their family. I was living like a gypsy, a few days here and a few days there.

Whilst staying with these families I become friends with their older siblings. It was fun at first as the older girls showed me how to dress and apply makeup. They made me feel beautiful. And then we were off to the nightclubs. Back then it was easy to get into night clubs. All you had to do was just look good, and older of course.

Reaching out from hell
A life full of pain and misery, feeling trapped in your
own hell. And yet there is a hope in your own higher
power to reach and ask for help.

Passion for music

I have a passion for music. I love any kind of music from pop to classical, in any language. The only music I don't like is heavy metal and rap.

When at a nightclub, I would dance and dance. The music was like a chant. When I was on that dance floor, my head down, hair on my face, eyes closed, I went with the music. It entered me, was me, merging with my heartbeat. The world was a dance floor, or

PART THREE – THE WILD YEARS

the dancefloor was my world. There is no one, just me, the music, and of course, alcohol. I had started to drink a lot of alcohol, and the taking of hallucinogens – these took me out of my mind.

Often, when I was dancing, I could feel many eyes on me. I didn't mind. I would open my eyes from time to time and check if there was some idiot behind me trying to do dirty dancing behind my back. When I found one, I would use my elbow and whacked him hard in the chest. That usually worked.

There was one nightclub that I often went to. I was well known to the bouncers, bartenders, and waitresses there. They knew I loved to dance by myself, they always look after me and kept me safe.

Prince charming

I was partying hard and virtually living in nightclubs, I met this charming man. I'll call him Prince Charming, just because of his big beautiful brown eyes and gorgeous smile. But Prince Charming came with demons. I was not even sixteen years old – he was in his early thirties when we became involved romantically. And with his warm smile I felt protected and understood. How wrong was I.

Prince Charming wanted to be a gangster. When I met him, he was hanging around with shady characters. Not just any gangster... He wanted to be a gang leader. He got involved with some bikie gangster bullshit where he had to prove himself and his worth. But he made me feel like a princess as he took me under his wing. I felt loved and important! No one could fuck with me... I was his woman.

One day, I'll never forget that day... I was at his house when he came home with a few of his thug-mates. Onto the kitchen table he dumped a lump of cocaine the size of a brick. Mind you, I'm a

3

kid, and this is happening in front of me. They were all happy and started digging into the cocaine. I didn't understand what was said or what was happening. It was my first experience of taking cocaine. Holy crap, I thought my face would fall off it was so numb. But it was a great feeling, at first.

Suddenly, there was loud banging on the door. I crapped myself. Prince Charming told me to go downstairs. The way the house was built, from the street it looked like a one level house. And from within, when you entered the house, you walked into the lounge room and so it still seemed to be single story. The stairway was not easily noticed. Anyway, I grabbed my little kitten and ran downstairs, holding it tight to my chest. I hid behind some cardboard boxes, hoping no one would find me. Next, there was screaming and shouting, and I am pretty sure a gunshot. There was a lot of scuffling of feet and thumping on the floor, like things were being dropped or dragged.

That scenario lasted a couple hours. Behind the boxes, I shivered in fright, and dared not to move. I had no idea what was going on upstairs. Then all went quiet but I still hid for another hour or so. Only then did I go and have a look. The house was empty.

I didn't understand what went on in that time. But looking back, I think that was his way of proving himself to the gangsters in his quest to assert himself as a criminal. Sort of like the Godfather. Wishful thinking! Now that bastard is in jail for murder. Thank God it was not my murder, or that no one knew I was there. When he was angry with me, he would be violent and shout at me.

Once, when I found out he was screwing another woman I picked up a plate and threw it at him, well not at him, at the wall close to him. He grabbed me by my hair and threw me down on the floor and started bashing my head against the floor. When I wanted to leave him, I went to the police to put an affidavit on him. That was a bad fucking idea. I woke up with the cold heavy metal of a gun against my forehead. When I opened my eyes he said, "Take that avo off me or I'll kill you!"

I was terrified and had no choice but to go to the police and withdraw it. Anyway, back to his house, I grabbed my cat and I called a taxi to go to a friend's home. I wondered where Prince Charming was or what had happened. The next day he told me that everything is okay. He did not tell me what happened, and quite frankly I did not want to know.

Filthy mistake

I dreamt big when I was a teenager. The dreams I had was to be a model/actor, lawyer, or doctor. You read above how I was forced out of home and how I left school, so how could I do those things? Nevertheless, I still managed to sign up with a modelling/acting agency. I cannot remember their name but I scored an acting role as an extra. The show was called Police Rescue (I think). For this scene, the cops found a dead body.

I, and a male actor, were in the background, observing police work, as if we were boy and girlfriend. We had no lines to say, which was good in a way as my English was a problem. Doing this scene was fun but it was my only role as an actress.

I continued trying to gain modelling jobs, but again my bad English was an obstacle. Over the years it improved, but when it came to reading and writing in English, it was not good.

Prince Charming knew of my desire to be a model. Before my sixteenth birthday, he offered to do a photo shoot of me for my modelling portfolio. To have a portfolio done through an agency would cost me far more money than I had.

We decided to do the shoot in a park. The one we selected

3

was beautiful with deep greenery, dancing flowers, and even a little creek flowing by. I took along nice clothes and lingerie. I was thrilled as it felt like a real modelling photo shoot. As there was no one around, we decided to take some nude photos, just for ourselves. I did not mind and felt comfortable doing so, after all he was my boyfriend.

We decided to do more photos (to expand my portfolio), but this time in a factory that he rented. There was a pool table which we used, me in sexy lingerie on top of the pool table.

In the end we had over 100 photos and I thought they looked good. After the shoot I bought myself a folder to display my portfolio. With this in hand I called many agencies, but most wanted the portfolio to be made by them so they disregarded me. Also, because of my poor English they did not even hear me out and often put the phone down. So rude, I was crushed.

Then one day Prince Charming said to me, "There's a competition in this magazine. You can be on the front cover and get paid $1500. But", he then paused for moment before continuing, "you would have to be naked". I was so excited and told him that was okay as I see a woman's body as a work of art, no matter what sort of figure the woman has.

Together we went through the photos that he took of me, wondering which we should send to the magazine? There was this one photo of me in lingerie on the pool table. That was the photo I decide to send.

Before sending, I needed to fill out the entrance form for the competition. Prince Charming helped me with this. He asked me questions, such as what hobbies do I like – what I do for fun – what my name is and where did I come from. The photo and the form were sent to the magazine. I had no idea what sort of magazine it was...

PART THREE – THE WILD YEARS

Two weeks later they phoned me and told me, "You are the winner. You are going to be on the front cover... When can you come in for an interview?" They also asked me to bring photos of me when I was younger.

I was excited and full of hope and that finally my modelling career was starting. After the phone call I told Prince Charming who whooped in delight. I ask him to come with me to the interview as I was nervous and needed him to help with the communication in case I did not understand something.

When we arrived for the interview, my heart was pounding like crazy. When I get nervous I need to pee, now! But first we introduced ourselves. As my nerves got the better of me, I excused myself to go to the toilet. When I came back the atmosphere was different. There were two men representatives for the magazine, plus Prince Charming – I can only think that they colluded in some sort of plan. But I only considered that later.

One of the men was quiet. He was just sitting observing me with a look of concern – he seemed worried. The other man was like a dog on heat. He was the one leading the interview and asked all the questions. The interview started okay with questions like what: you do you like for fun – where do you come from – how long have you been in Australia – do you read our magazines, which I said no, but now I will because I'm in it. Then the sexual questions started: which female actor would you like to have sex with – which male actor would you like to have sex with – what is your favourite sex position – what is your sexual fantasy – which animal would you have sex with – what do you do in the bedroom with your boyfriend – do you like girls?
As he asked me these questions, I could see he was aroused. This made me feel uneasy, especially because my boyfriend was listening.

The questions ended and then he showed me a bunch of photos, all disgusting pictures of ugly penises. He asked me which one

3

is a good-looking one, and which one is not to my taste. I had to tell him what I thought about them. Before answering, I ask why he wants this information? His answer, "Oh, just to see what you think, no problem".

When the interview was finished I had to sign a contract. I asked them what am I signing? His answer was, "So we can publish your story and pictures", which I assumed was going to only be for one edition of the magazine. They could see I could not read English.

At that time I was nearly seventeen and the photo I sent to competition was when I was fifteen. They never asked me my age. From the beginning I had a bad feeling about all of this but being young, and overly keen I did not want to see those red flags.

I was told by them, that Id' be doing a photoshoot with a professional photographer. She was a nice lady and very professional, with a nice studio. She did my hair and make-up and advised me what to wear and which lingerie should I wear. She also told me how to pose for the photos. I had so much fun doing the photo shoot. She made me feel beautiful and comfortable and felt I was on my way as a model. I have wondered about this lady and if she was part of their scheming, that perhaps she was just another cog in the wheel, but she seemed so nice.

After the photoshoot I had to sign another contract with her. When I asked what this one was for, she replied, "So I have permission to release your photos to magazine". I was over the moon. My first professional photoshoot and for a magazine. And front cover!

Not long after that photoshoot the magazine called and told me I had to do another photoshoot, but this time for a graphic (comic) story. I was pleased that they wanted me again.

When the first magazine came out, because I could not read English, I had to ask a girlfriend to read it to me. Maria read it but did not want to tell me everything that was in it. I pushed her to tell

PART THREE – THE WILD YEARS

me exactly what was written. On the first page of the magazine, there I was in a nice pose but written next to it was a crap and cryptic joke, *Anna Partridge in a pear tree….Ha ha ha.* They had twisted my name. There were disgusting stories about me as they knew I did not read English and therefore were free to print whatever the hell they wanted. There were racist remarks about me. From that one photoshoot they use my pictures in their magazines at least seven times in different articles. Then, later I found out I was in a different pornographic magazine. I have no idea how many of these they had me in.

I found out through friends that each time the magazine came out, I was in it. Then one day one of my friends phoned me and told me, "You are in that magazine again". I went and purchased a copy to see for myself. When I looked through the magazine, there I was!… surrounded with all those penises along with my opinion of them. I thought to myself this fucking pig lied to me in the interview. I was so angry.

I decided to sue them so started looking for lawyers to help me. Most of them did not want to take my case, because they were worried about the opposite side – meaning they did not have the balls to take this case because that magazine had the best lawyers, barristers, power, and the money. Also, most of them did not believe me, even though I had all the magazines as proof. Most of the lawyers I spoke to over the phone told me to go to the police. I did not want to go to the police because I was ashamed, and I didn't want to be judged by them.

For years I searched for lawyers to help me get financial justice and remove the magazines from public view. I found one lawyer who agreed to have an appointment at his at his office in Sydney's CBD. I took along all the magazines. The meeting lasted half an hour and finished with him suggesting I leave the magazines with him, and to make another appointment to see him a week later to follow-up.

3

In the meantime, I called the magazine and told them to stop publishing me and that I was underage at that time. A week later I returned to the lawyer's reception but the receptionist replied, "No one by that name works here." She appeared to have no knowledge of that person and said there is no record of my appointment of last week. I knew and I felt in my heart that he got paid to disappear, and with my magazines. Deflated, I had no evidence and those bastards are getting away with it.

As the years passed the magazine haunted me as friends told me that the magazine is still in a public view. I decided to go to that library and see for myself. When there I took photos of the magazine as my proof. In a way I was happy and relieved because I had all the evidence back in my hands. But at the same time, my blood was boiling and my head was pounding hard and loud. I felt rage and humiliated. My English reading had improved enough to make out what was printed in the magazine. This was the first time without having to ask friends to read it for me. In one issue what I saw was shocking. I quote their words, ...*naked with children...* this was in respect to a photo of a mother, grandmother, and a naked baby in the middle. I had to stop for a moment and had a long stare at that story. The editor of that particular story had written, *Even though the gutsy trio lived in WA they avoided being detected by authorities and smuggled their photo to our office* – it was as clear as day and made me sick. The sorry fact is that this magazine can get away with murder and bribes and no one will do anything about it.

When finding out that the magazines was still in public view I lapsed into my addiction of alcohol, pot, whilst being on depression tablets. This combination is a disaster for a breakdown. But I still looked for lawyers but always getting the same outcome, where they did not believe me or did not have the balls to fight the magazine.

Finally, I decided to go to the police. Being nervous I got high on pot for courage and to numb the shame. I arrived with all the photos of the magazines I had collected, including the stories about naked babies in the pornographic magazine.

The detective who interviewed me was young, in his thirties. He was power driven. When I reported my story, he sniffed something bigger and was only interested in Prince Charming's role in this, instead of seeing the bigger picture, CHILDREN AND BABIES in a pornographic situation! I did not finish the statement with him that day. It was too much, I was shaking and needed a cone badly, so as to forget that shit and to calm down.

The next day I admitted myself to rehab. I wanted, and needed to be with it if I was going to tell my story to the police. I had to be clear headed and strong. When in rehab, I became friendly with one of the clients, Mark. I told him about my story with the magazine, and also the copper that I saw. When I told Mark about Prince Charming, he said to me, "This cop will get you killed if he just wants to go after Prince Charming. Don't go back to him. I know a lawyer and I will call him for you." Which he did and organised a meeting once I got out of recovery. Once again, I had the hope of a lawyer that will hear me out and maybe take my case.

When I showed up to the new lawyer, he was nice and seems to be genuine. His name was Steve. He asked me if it is okay to record our meeting on a recorder. I did not mine. When I was telling him about the lawyer that disappeared with my magazines he instantly stopped recording and said, "This is like in the movies". I got angry thinking he was taking piss out of me. It is my life, not a fucking movie. Then he warned, "This is a very difficult case. But I'll help you get justice." Then, out of respect for me, he asked me to cover up all the naked pictures of me.

I told him everything, that they publish whatever they wanted about me and when they wanted. They even publish my actual full name. When I compared this to articles using other girls, they did not have their surname shown, and the stories were more respect-

3

ful. What they had written about me was disgusting, that I lived for booze, drugs and fucking. They used me, exploited me, they lied to me, assassinated my character, betraying me as a slut. They took advantage of my young, gullible age, took advantage of my lack of reading and writing in English.

It was around this time that I that was so distraught, that I started dissociating. I could not drive my car as when driving I went through red lights without realising. At one time my daughter Suzanna was with me and shouted, "Watch out" and if it wasn't for her, I probably would have a smash into another car. It was like my body was there, but my mind was completely blank. I could not see what was going on around me I just had tunnel vision.

The stress got to me and on one occasion when the girls were not home I got blood pressure pills and a bottle of spirits, which I drank straight. I placed all the pills (about 100) on the coffee table, ready to take as I just wanted to fall asleep and never wake up. Then something told me to get another bottle because one wasn't enough. Again, I went to the bottle shop and got another bottle of spirits. I think that last bottle saved my ass because whilst drinking it I blacked out without having the pills.

When I woke up the next day, I saw those pills all over the coffee table. It really scared me. If it wasn't for that second bottle, I probably would have popped those pills.

Frantic, I phoned my counsellor. Desperately begging her to see her that very day. When I saw her I told her what I had done, as well as telling her that I am here but I'm not here. I could not feel my soul, my mind, my thoughts nothing – I am numb. She advised me to immediately book into the hospital's mental unit. She would call so they knew I was coming in.

After being admitted the doctor put me on new medication that was antipsychotic. I was in that mental unit for four weeks.

PART THREE – THE WILD YEARS

When I saw Steve for the second time, I told him what I wanted. At first, I wanted eight million dollars. OK, maybe that was not realistic but remember it was a pornographic magazine with a minor being used, exploited, shamed and ridiculed. Plus, I wanted the magazine to be removed from a public view. Steve told me I would never get eight million and it is unlikely they will remove the magazines from public view. I asked him to ask for four million. Steve said that if we go to court I will lose because of Mr X (Prince Charming). He explained that the people from magazine would blame Mr X who encouraged me to go on that interview, took me to the interview, and that he took pictures of me, aged fifteen. What kind of law and justice is that?

I was pissed off with Steve. This magazine paid off one lawyer to disappear with my magazines. They used me, expose me, they lied to me regarding the contract, they insulted me! And here he is telling me I have no case.... Extortion, exploiting young children in a pornographic magazine, all the humiliation, disgusting stories about me, dicks plastered all over my face or should I say around my face, revealing my surname and more. For instance, when I was trying to get modelling jobs, as soon I mentioned that agency and the magazine that I modelled in, they politely rejected me and told me, "No thank you".

Now, if I was a detective, the first thing that I would like to see is the account for the magazine. I am pretty sure they would find traces of secret payment to the lawyer that disappeared.

When I argued with Steve not seeing the bigger picture and how serious this was, why would he not do what I asked of him. So he fired me, and his excuse was, "I'm not going to do your case for two reasons. I'm worried about Mr X coming after you and your daughters, and the second reason is that they will never remove those magazines from public view."

When I got stronger mentally, I again looked for a lawyer and had few meetings. Before I could organise a face-to-face meeting, I

3

spoke with them over the phone, telling them roughly what is going on with my case and that my last lawyer dumped me. Their answers were: We don't do criminal cases – we are a small company and we do not have the resources – you need to go to the police". Again, they tell me to go to the police.

I decided to go to the cops once again. This time sober and with a clear head, where I met a lovely detective. His surrounding aura was light blue and I felt him fair and respectful towards me – he was very professional. I told him everything. But unfortunately, once again this detective was more interested in Mr X (Prince charming). That first day I spent at least two hours with him. I saw him maybe three times to finish the statement. Once finished, he said, "You have to sign this statement and remember once you sign that you are going to be in the witness box to testify. And Mr X will be charged with child pornography pictures."

But Prince Charming is not someone to fuck around with. I did not sign the statement as I feared that once he learns about this charge towards him, he would come after me or my children. Even though he was in prison, he has people on the outside.

So I was back to square one, looking for lawyers again. I found one lady lawyer and made an appointment to see her. She commiserated with me but was a one lawyer company and too small an outfit. She did not even have a receptionist. She said to me she could not take my case, because she was operating on her own. She did not have enough funds or resources for my type of case. I asked her if she could write a letter to Steve to reconsider and take my case on. She did write that letter.

When I called Steve to ask him to take me back, he agreed but told me that I would be paying him out from the settlement – there would be no court case. I asked him why he can't make the other side pay my legal fees, after all, if it wasn't for them, I would not be in this situation.

Steve never told me what he was going to ask for or what his fee was to be. When I asked him how much are you going to ask for, he did not give a proper answer. All he said was, "You'll be lucky if you get a $1 million from victim's compensation". Surprisingly, Steve says he does not remember saying that to me. It's interesting to me how some lawyers only remember what suits them. If I did get one million then I would settle with that.

Then Steve called me with good news telling me that we had a settlement date which was sometime in June 2022. After five long years of me putting the evidence together, having been hospitalised twice in mental units, going through psychiatrists, counsellors and suicide attempts I hoped it would show them what they have put me through.

Steve was excited about it but at the same time he wore his mask. Every lawyer or barrister wears a mask. The question is which mask are they wearing today? In my opinion all lawyers wear a mask, to make it hard to read what they are thinking. Most of them have sold their souls to the devil and they don't even know it! Amongst the evil there are few little angles.

Anyway… I asked Steve to see me before that settlement day. When I got to his office I was really nervous as I did not know what to expect from him. I had asked Steve to ask for two million dollars but would settle for one million. He said that "can't happen. I can probably get between $200,000-$300,000 may be $100,000 if you're lucky. But you have to take it no matter what they offer for you. Just take it! You owe me $20,000 already". $20,000 for what!?

Before we finished our meeting, he asked me if I had received the estimate of how much I can get? I replied I have not received an email with such information. As we finished our meeting, he said he would tell me later what he would be asking for. That never happened.

3

Before the settlement day I wrote down what I would like to say to them in the meeting. Sort of like a Victim's Impact Statement.

This is what I wrote: (Editor's note. To give you the full impact of Anna's writing ability it is presented as written)

First of all, I do not know what contract I have signed with magazine. And when I asked what am signing, he said "so we can publish your story and pictures" assuming it's going to be only one magazine with me in it at that time. As well I was never asked about my age.

Then during the interview I was asked revolting questions and showed all the ugly penises to pick the one that is good-looking and the one that I think is the worst. When I asked why they wanted me to pick which penis is good-looking and which one is bad. The answer was "we just want to see what you think about them" and then later learning and seeing my face surrounded with penises all around me in the magazine. Without letting me know that there would be more magazines with me in it. I felt angry, rage and disgusted it.

Use my child communion photo which I provided. Thinking that the story that would be written about me and that would be the beginning of my modelling career. From a young child turning into a beautiful young lady.

Twisting my words to write more filthy stories about me. Totally taken advantage of my lack of knowledge in English. And not to be able to read or write in English at all at that time.

Questions "what animals would you have sex with?" Most of the questions made me feel uneasy and confused. Why would they ask me such filthy questions?

When I was putting my evidence together, I read properly what was written about me instead of asking my friends to read it to me. And to my understanding it was written and suggested that I had

PART THREE – THE WILD YEARS

sex with the interviewer, after the interview. And that he will write more in the next article about what happens when he "gets back to earth". And that was one of the quotes made in a magazine. When I read what was said about me and what I saw was more disturbing stories and pictures of babies. I felt my blood boiling once again. Which lead me to have a breakdown and suicide attempt.

I looked for lawyers to help me and get my justice financially as the magazine made millions on my expense. Most did not believe me what had happened to me. I was advised to go to the police. Advised by the lawyers that did not believe me. I did not want to go to the police because I felt shame and fear of being judged.

I finally find one lawyer that would talk to me face-to-face. I had brought all my magazines to this meeting with him. After the meeting I left a magazine with him. And made an appointment to see him the following week. In the meantime I have made call to the magazine and told them to stop printing magazines with me in it and that I was underage.

When I showed up the next week to see the lawyer again. The receptionist did not have me in the book appointment at all, and said that the lawyer I was asking for did not work there. She never heard or had any knowledge of that person. He just disappeared with my magazine as my proof. I thought to myself that it must've paid off and all my magazines are gone. I felt disregarded, hopeless, unrepresented and I felt sadness. Know I have a good lawyer with me and I know I am not standing alone.

And once again few years goes by. My old friend told me that the magazines are still in public view till this day. Pictures of me as a young child and underage teenager in pornographic magazines, with my surname that anyone can look me up. I do not go a lot to social media, because I am afraid to see something that is about me not in a nice way. Or maybe some weird weirdo is looking for me through Google search.

3

I felt anger, hurt, frustrated, defeated, sad and mentally exhausted!

I have been humiliated, racism marks were written about me, been called stupid and a "crappy joke Hehe" you have exploited me, used me, insulted me, take advantage of my young age, taken advantage of my luck of English reading and writing skills, printing my full name in the magazine and I compared to the other girls in that magazine and did not had their full name printed in magazine only me.

I feel exposed, used, abused and angry each time I am reminded of this magazine.

I am a mother now with two very different daughters to each other. They are my reminder of how gullible and naive that age was for me and the dreams that I had as a young girl.

I knew I had to pose naked, but I see beauty in a naked woman's body after all I am an artist by trade. And I had no idea how perverted and disgusting that magazine was or should I say it is.

Put yourself in my shoes when I was 16 to 17 years old. We were young once before. Thinking I know it all, how to impress a boy or girl, how to fit in, how to be accepted and how do you talk with your parents when you are in trouble.

I had no one to be there for me. And by having my justice met. I can give my girls what I never had. Security, comfort and most of all that you can trust the universe to do the right thing by you. And in all fairness if you have daughters and day when taken advantage of sexually and been exploited. Where would the perpetrators stand in your eyes?

Thank you so much for hearing me out and hoping that I will meet my justice today. I have written a book because I feel my story should be told to the world. However if my justice is served I can move on and take this chapter out of my book and therefore out of my life. Thank you for your time.

PART THREE – THE WILD YEARS

After my speech they were quiet for a moment. One of the guys from the magazine apologised. He said they are very sorry for what has happened to me and that it should not have happened. He sounded sincere, but that apology was no good to me because the damage to me has already been done. I wanted compensation and the removal of those magazines from public view.

Then one lady lawyer representing the magazine took over and said, in big-lawyers' words something like, "This was done such a long time ago we don't have any records regarding your contract or any information... so the case is prejudice". Whatever the fuck does that means? But I know why, *you got rid of all of the evidence when I called to the magazine and told them I was underage. You even paid that lawyer to disappear.*

Then they said to us, "We have given you our offer. We will leave the room so you can discuss what your decision will be. We will be next door".

Once they left the room, Steve showed me a piece of paper, where on it was written how much he was going to ask for. This was between $294,440.00 to $391,180.00 for the compensation. But then he told me that their offer was for $100 000. I was unhappy about this and told him. So, he went next door, without me, to discuss it with them. Each time he returned saying they would not budge, that their maximum is $100,000. Steve asked, "What do you want to do?"
I said I have no way out and you won't go to court with me?
"No" Steve replied, "and you owe me $60,000 but I will give you a discount. You can pay me $40,000. I thought what the fuck? From a couple of months ago before the settlement he told me I owed him $20 000. Now it is $60 000! And he is doing me a big favour by taking $20 000 off as a discount. These are the thoughts that were screaming in my head.
"Take what they are offering you and this can be over".

69

3

I could hear them next door laughing and giggling. Like this matter was a joke to them.

I felt trapped and cornered. Steve was paid $100 000 and gave me $60 000. But the magazine is still out there in the public view. On top of that the removal of the magazines from public view was not mentioned at all.

I wondered about Steve's part in this. I have no doubt that if I had the money, and if Prince Charming was not about, then I could have had Steve disbarred as a lawyer. It would not surprise me if they also paid him an amount over and above the $100 000, to shut me up. I was exhausted, but still want to expose them for what they are.

One way or another people will know my story. I have not mentioned their names or the magazine name. Steve's name is made up. But having my book out there with my story, hoping that someone takes this seriously and changes the law. Punishable by death. Yes, it is little bit dramatic, but think about it – all those sexually abused children. They will never have a proper life, relationships or good job. Most of them turn to drugs or booze to escape the pain. Sadly, most people tend to judge the abused without even knowing what sort of life they had. Shame on us.

Exotic dancer

I had to do something for money to survive and have a place to live. I called these, 'the golden years' because I loved dancing, and got paid well for doing so. But these golden years led to darkness.

As the song goes "...and everybody knows". When I became an exotic dancer there was a lot of cocaine, drugs, and parties as I could not do it straight, meaning sober. I was drinking heavily and taking lots of drugs. I needed them to have the courage to get on

PART THREE — THE WILD YEARS

the dance floor and start stripping, and to get through each day. At the beginning it was new and exciting, and I was always high in one way or another.

When I was on the stage, I had power. Because of the bouncers, no one could touch me, they could only look. I felt like a goddess up there. It was intoxicating knowing that every eye was on me and knowing that at the same time what they were thinking. But they could do nothing about it other than giving me dollars so I would get closer to them and teased the crap out of them.

Can't touch this

As an exotic dancer you deal with all sorts of people, weird people, funny people, shy people, and of course perverts. Back then it was classier as you only stripped down to your G-string. If anyone wanted to see the full Monty, there were private rooms for that. But still no touching. Private rooms bought more money for me and the club.

Some of them came for fun, excitement, entertainment, and some just because they were lonely and wanted company. The best and worst traits of those men came out when drunk.

One night a young man showed up. He looks like he came from Wall Street in his expensive suit, shiny shoes, and expensive watch. He was shy and quiet. Just my cup of tea. He was in a large crowd of mainly men, but I started seducing him with my eyes and movement. Finally, he agreed to have a private show with me.

In the private room I sat him down while I danced just in front of him, slowly stripping. I teased him, slowly removing my lingerie. Using my hands in slow rhythm. I gently stroked my breasts, my hips, my thighs. I could see the young man was getting 'hot'. I also got aroused. I came up close to him and started rubbing myself with my ass against his groin. I felt his hard penis against my body. Then I felt wetness on his lap – he had come in his pants.

That was a satisfying feeling, seeing him getting off on me just by watching my performance. I felt like I was the goddess, untouchable with the power I had over him.

NOW you're fucked!

I had this other guy hassling me for sex. But at that time I was the hostess of the club. He was a persistent bastard, and annoying.

I told him, "Okay. I'll fuck you for 200 bucks". That was a lot of money those days. He gave me the $200, and then I told him. "Now! You're fucked." He went to my manager and told him that I ripped him off for $200. My manager was a good guy and looked after the girls. Most of all he was understanding and fair. My boss came to me and told me to give him $150 back and keep $50 as a lesson to him. The customer came back to me, and I gave him the $150. When he asked, "Where's the other $50?"

"I'm keeping it to teach you a lesson, so you'll never hassle me again. If you got a problem with that, go to the manager." He got embarrassed and left the club like a dog with a tail between his legs.

Asian tour

From time to time, we would have tourists come to the club for a show, on their own or in tour groups. I was a cheeky dancer and could handle a tough crowd or in some cases a weird crowd.

When we had Asian tour groups, I was the one who would entertain them in one of the private rooms. Oh boy, let me tell you the reaction of the Asian men and women towards the naked body of a white woman.

It's like we are aliens. They would poke me with their fingers, whilst whispering to each other. They pointed and when I came closer to them, they would shove their fingers in my butt and try to manhandle my breasts in a rough manner, like they were examining rotten meat at the market. Both men and women. I was an object that needed to be touched just to see if it's real.

Then you get the other type of Asian group. Totally different behaviour. Shy, quiet, and reserved, keeping their hands to themselves. I preferred this group because I could have fun with them. I would tease them and get right-up close to them to see their embarrassment. When I did, they giggled and talked loudly among themselves. Even more so when I picked one of their men to do a laptop dance on. Or pick a woman who seemed shyer but intrigued with a white woman's breasts. Then that person would get excruciatingly embarrassed – with a red face they would fidget and cover their face with their hands. The rest would giggle or laugh as they jabbered in their language. I was entertainment for them, and it was all good fun.

Double Trouble – the twins

There was one man who constantly hassled me for sex. He offered money which I did not accept. I had no interest in him. I told him, "If you want a fuck, go to a brothel."
He kept on at me for at least a year. One day he came in with his twin brother. When I saw both, the kinky side of me came out. I said, "You, and you, with me home!"
They were stunned at the thought of a threesome but could not get me out fast enough.

It is amazing how two brothers can look the same but be totally different as lovers. The one that hassled me for sex was a selfish lover, rough and hopeless. He had no clue what he was doing. His brother was the opposite, gentle and caring, and made sure that I was satisfied before he finished. His name was Jimmy, and his brother's name was Jackass. His name is not even worth mentioning.

Jimmy and I had an immediate attraction to each other, not just physically but mentally. He became my boyfriend for two years. He was intelligent, kind, and funny. Unfortunately, I met this girl Lisa who had a strong influence over me. She convinced me to break up with Jimmy and not to let him back in my house. In my immaturity, and drinking and dope, I listened to her. I threw Jimmy's clothing and belongings through the window onto the street. When he came back from work I did not let him in. Lisa was with me at the time and said I should call the police to get rid of him. I did. I was cold, heartless, and unkind. Till this day I regret what I did to him. If I didn't listen to that bitch my life probably could be a whole different story. I never saw him again.

Fun club

There was a well-known nightclub called... well, I'll leave the name out, but it was like Studio 54, where entrance was limited to the famous, the beautiful, and rich folks. You are probably wondering how I got in? Well, Megan was a couple of years older than me and was a true beauty. Her background was Italian, and she had lovely golden-olive skin, a beautiful figure, long wavy hair, and big brown eyes. She was a bomb and knew how to operate any man with her charm and her beauty.

She told me how to dress and how to behave. All I had to do was to stand behind her, look beautiful, be confident, and follow her lead. Once in the nightclub we became separated, but that was

PART THREE – THE WILD YEARS

okay as I was a big girl. The place was pumping with good music, lots of alcohol, and of course drugs; cocaine, heroin, ecstasy, anything that you wanted you could get. I had my own drugs on me, but if you wanted more... My favourite drug was ecstasy. Back then the ecstasy was amazing. I would take half of the ecstasy, and dance on a dance floor for at least eight hours just on that one half tab.

I'm dancing away and having the time of my life. I got hot and thirsty so went to the bar for water. At the bar there was this guy, I don't know his name. That's not important, he was not important. He approached me and asked me if I wanted some ecstasy? I looked him up and down because I knew he thought to himself *if I give her ecstasy, she'll be mine*. He was wrong. I was glad to take his ecstasy but I made it clear to him that I was not going to have sex with him, just for that.

"Oh no... it's okay that's not what I want" he said. He probably thought to himself *once the ecstasy hits, she'll come to me*. This is because when on ecstasy you feel fantastic, in a loveable mood, and horny if the person is right. Plus, I never blacked out on ecstasy I always knew what I was doing.

I took it and left him at the bar. An hour later he came to me and asked, "How are you feeling?"
"Fantastic... I'm so enjoying your ecstasy. But I'm still not gonna fuck you!"
He became frustrated and looked at me with that look *I just wasted my good drugs on you bitch...*

Oh well what I can say, bye, bye next!...

Silent but deadly

In one of the clubs I worked, Tom worked in the same club as a cleaner. Sometimes he worked behind the bar serving drinks. He

3

was quiet, softly spoken, a bit shy and looked after the girls. For example, he would go and get us food when we wanted. And of course, cleaning the club at the end of the night.

One night I was drunk, as usual, and started to walk home when Tom appears from club back entrance of the club. When he saw me, he offered to walk home with me, as if he was some sort of bodyguard. Because I knew him from the club, I assumed I would be safe walking home with him. My apartment was just few streets away.

Being drunk, I couldn't walk straight, so Tom held me as we walked. Once we got closer to my apartment I blacked out. I don't remember if Tom came up for coffee, or if I invited him.

The next day I woke up with a pain in my ass. I knew he raped me in my butt. I have never tried or wanted anal sex. And I knew in my heart that I wouldn't ask for that.

I couldn't prove what happened to me with Tom. Plus, I was ashamed and embarrassed. I did not speak to Tom about it. I did not tell anyone what happened. Who would believe me?

When you work in sex industry as an erotic dancer or a prostitute, it's pointless going to the police to tell them that you've been raped. Society does not see those girls as human beings. And yet, when men go to those clubs or brothels, they find consolation and share their problems and stories. Some would just come in as perverts.

The next night when I went to work, I avoided Tom and did not make eye contact. Once I did my show, I went straight to the girls dressing room. Tom was not allowed to enter the girls dressing room. I knew I'd be safe if I stayed out of his way. I did not want to face him or have anything to do with him.

At that time, I was going out with the boss, Alex. He would lose

PART THREE – THE WILD YEARS

his shit and probably would bash the hell out of Tom, or worse if he knew.

Alex noticed my strange behaviour towards Tom. He asked me if anything happened between me and Tom and why I seemed to be avoiding him? Why am I saying such cold words to Tom?

If I was nasty or revengeful all I had to do was to tell Alex what happened, and that bastard would have what's coming to him. Everyone knew I was Alex's girl, and you don't fuck with Alex. I told Alex, "That Tom said something stupid and offensive to me and I just do not like the guy anymore. And why should I give him my time if he does not have proper manners." Thank God Alex believed my story and left it alone.

Unfortunately, Alex passed away. The story was that he had a heart attack and choked on his tongue. But he had many enemies, I don't believe that story. I have a strong feeling that he was murdered. Fortunately, I was not with him at the time of his death and had already moved on with my life and left stripping behind me.

*Forbidden to see.
Represents queen of fire. No one should see her. But if you catch her staring at the candle flame, you see she is fragile and beautiful. Yet she holds power and string of life.*

Trafficking in 'green vegetable' matter

One time I was pissed and made my way to the police station. In my drunken state I had a fetish for boys in a blue uniform. I thought I'd just pop in and ask a cop for a fuck. That should be easy enough I thought.

When I arrived at the counter, I ask, "So who's gonna to fuck me tonight?"
They laughed and told me to go home.

PART THREE – THE WILD YEARS

"I'm not going anywhere until I get what I want". Then I blacked out.

The next day I woke up in a police cell. They charged me with three charges. First, for refusing a breathalyser. Second; offensive language in a public place. Third; I was charged with... wait for it... 'Trafficking with green vegetable matter'.

What the fuck?! I had no idea what this third charge was. I did have half a joint on me at the time but I *never* sold drugs. I was scared because trafficking is a jailable offence. Seems that because I was a bitch to them, they decided to teach me a lesson.

When it came to the court day, I'll never forget the judge's face. He looked down at the charge sheet and read it out loud. Suddenly stopping and asking, "What are these ridiculous charges... trafficking with green vegetable matter... ... what did she have, a cucumber?!" When I heard that I almost pissed myself laughing. The judge looked at the cops and said, "Don't waste my time with such rubbish."

For the two other charges I got off with a good behaviour bond for twelve months. That was my first encounter with the police. But! Wait there's more. Several more, actually.

Blow me

I was driving back home from a party. It was 2:00 in the morning. I did not drink at the party, but I did have some pot. Before I left the party, I cleaned my mouth with Listerine, so I didn't smell like pot.

I'm driving slowly and carefully towards home when suddenly I hear a siren behind me. Cops!! I pulled over. As I sat in my car waiting for them to come to my window, I was nervous, even

though back then they did not have on the spot drug testing, only breathalysing. Two officers got out of the car. One was young, the other was older. The younger officer asked me the questions.
"Have you been drinking today?"
"No. not today... or tonight."
He stuck a breathalyser in my hand and said blow and keep doing so for a count of ten. He counted as I blew. When I finished, he checked the reading and says, "It shows that you have had alcohol."
"No officer. I have not had any drinks tonight." I explained that I had used Listerine to clean my mouth before I left my friends. Listerine is alcohol based.
He replied, "Let's try another tester. Once again blow until ten". Again, I blow. Once finished I asked the young officer, "Is there anything else you want me to blow?" I said that to him in a 'very chick' and a smartass way.

The officer became flustered and did not know what to say. The older cop stepped in and shone his torch in my face. He asked me for my ID and what I was doing driving so late. I explained that I had visited friends, had nothing to drink there, and was now returning home. They didn't charge me with anything and let me go. But I'm sure that 'blow' comment spread across the police station like a plague. I was becoming known to the local cops.

Safe speed limit

It's a beautiful day, and I'm driving the freeway. I'm cruising along at 110 km/h, the speed limit. A police car drove past me and so I decided to drive behind it. He was driving much faster than I was. I sped up to the same speed and hit 140 km/h, which was 30 km/h over the limit. I followed him until I approached my exit, when I slowed down to the correct exit speed. The policeman, seeing me leaving the highway, turned around to follow me.

PART THREE – THE WILD YEARS

Once he caught up, he signalled for me to pull over. I was wondering,

what now?
He was pissed off.
I slide my window down and asked him, "Why have you pulled me over?"
His reply, "Why were you following me?"
I answered him with my cheeky voice, "Well... is it not safe to follow a police officer?"
In a threatening way he responded, "You know you were doing 130 km/h?"
"Actually officer, I was doing 140 km/h, and so were you."
He nearly exploded with anger. It looked like he had steam coming out of his ears. "You know I can book you for that and you can lose your license!"
I replied, "You can't fine me for speeding as I was driving behind you at your speed."
He asked me for my driving license. I had a valid license but did not have it on me. He gave me a fine for driving without having my license with me. He had to let off steam so gave me the ticket. Back then they did not have cameras at the back of the police car. Not only that, but he would also have got into trouble, possibly losing his job. It was fun driving behind him. But most of all, it was satisfactory to me that he was in the wrong. And he couldn't do anything about it.

Let me pee

Once again I was drunk, this time in a pub, where I refused to leave the premises when asked to leave. The manager called the police. I had no idea because I was sitting playing a poker machine. Then, from behind me I hear a voice asking me to get up and leave the premises. When I turned around there were two cops. I got up and started to leave without resistance. Even so, these police officers were rude and aggressive. They grabbed me by my arms, one either side and started dragging me towards the police van. I was wearing high heels, so by their rough handling I could not walk properly. They half dragged me to the Paddy Wagon and pushed me in the back, like I was a sack of potatoes, and locked the door.

Driving to the police station they drove fast and bounced me around in the back. There are no seat belts or handles in those boxes to hang onto. I was like a pea in a whistle as I rolled and banged with each corner. First this way, then that way. They roughed me up pretty damn good and I had bruises afterwards, where I looked like I had been in a catfight, but not with the woman, a man.

When we got to the police station, they locked me up in the cell with a metal bed. The cell was cold. In a corner there was a toilet, also made of cold metal. Just behind and above the toilet was a camera.

I really needed to go to the toilet. I called out for someone to come and get me and take me to the toilet. Instead of one officer coming to my cell, they all came. They told me to do my business in the toilet in my cell, with them and the camera watching. I was to be their entertainment.

I was humiliated, and angry with these seven or eight cops, including a few lady cops standing in front of my cell, watching. They joked and laughed, whilst pointing at me like I was some sort of monkey. Motherfuckers...

All for me?

Vicky, my neighbour, and friend was a partner in crime. We used to party hard together. We loved dressing up and going to the city

PART THREE – THE WILD YEARS

where we had lots of fun.

One night we were to meet friends in the city and drove my car at around 1;00 in the morning. The roads were dark and empty. No traffic whatsoever. Suddenly a car behind us flashes a high beam signalling me to pull over. Then the lights start flashing blue and red. I realised it was the police. Again.

I pulled over and sat quietly waiting for the policeman to approach my car.
"Do you know why I pulled you over?"
"I have no idea officer."
"Your car is out of registration. Please stay in your car, I am going to call for paperwork to give you a warning."

After about ten minutes he returned, "I'll let you off with a warning, but you cannot drive the car, until your registration is updated."

We made a phone call to our friends to come and pick us up. In the meantime, the officer went back to his car and sat there. Fifteen minutes later, they still sat there, which annoyed us.

Suddenly, there were loud police sirens of at least ten police cars, which surrounded us. They all got out of their car's and observed us. We were confused, what the hell's going on? Then the original officer that pulled us over came over to us with the official warning for me to sign. After this was done, he said, "Have you got somebody coming to pick you up?"
"Yes," I replied.

I couldn't understand why all these cops arrived in the middle of the night when I was only getting a warning. Then I work it out! They came for the show. The show of me. To see how I'm going to lose it and what other crazy shit I would say or do. Maybe I would offer to blow someone. Just kidding. But I would not be surprised if that's what they thought, *Oh she's the crazy nutter, let's see what other crazy shit she will do blah blah blah...*

I thought, *Sorry boys, not tonight. I'm a good girl, besides having my car not registered I could get into further trouble.*

21st century witch

I have spiritual gifts. Sometimes I think they are a curse. This is because there are good and bad spirits, and the bad ones scare me. Well... in terms of labels that people give us clairvoyants; sensitives, gifted, witch, psychic, mad or schizophrenia.

I am pretty sure I'm the first woman in the 21st century to have been charged with witchcraft. I am not joking! I had been charged with putting a hex on the officer who arrested me at that time. Even my lawyer had a good laugh when he read the charge to me... "She even put a hex on us..."

At that time, I didn't understand what 'hex' meant and asked my lawyer. He had a little giggle to himself and explained, "It's like putting a supernatural jinx, or juju on someone... it's like you put a spell on them."

"What did I do? I merely told each what I had seen in them." "You were bullied at school and so you become a police officer so you can take your frustration out on others." "You! You don't have brothers and sisters and you've been spoiled rotten, and you loved the power!" "You! Become a police officer because you believe in justice! So, keep your heart pure to your beliefs." "You! Tortured little animals because you have a god complex, and by becoming a police officer you hold the power of control." And... they freaked out, especially the policeman who was typing when I asked him. "So? Is she pregnant, yet?" I saw his wedding ring and that wedding ring showed me his wife trying to get pregnant with him. They had been trying for a while but had problems. He went totally white, got up from the desk and quickly went out the back so I could not see him. In a few seconds four police officers came out to see for themselves who that woman was. Their curiosity cost them embarrassment and shock once I told them what I saw. Then all of them left me alone and went back out. A few moments later the big chief comes out, pretending he's getting something from the printer, whilst quietly observing me from the side of his eyes. What I saw in him was scary. He had a dark aura around him, almost black. I told him. "You... you're evil, you get off on inflicting pain to others. You go to Brussels and abuse the prostitutes because you can. You are an evil man..." As I told him these things, I was calm because I was afraid of what I saw in him. All he said was "Yeah whatever" then quickly left for the back to where the rest of the police officers were. But I did see the fear in him and could see him for what he was.

It's not my fault that I am blessed with such a gift, but as I said before sometimes, they are cursed. It comes and goes, I see things before they happen, I can communicate with the other side – I see dead people , spirits. In other words, spirits. Sometimes I read people's minds, it just happens. I don't ask for it and cannot do it when someone puts me on the spot. But when it comes it can be overwhelming. I'll explain more about this later.

Meeting my guardian angel

Believe it or not but I met an angel in the exotic dancing industry. To me he is an angel. He is tall, athletic and has beautiful silver hair. He looked a bit like Indiana Jones.

From time to time he came with his friends, always, in an expensive suit and shoes. I could tell he was wealthy. He worked for an international company and was one of the top 100 partners in Australia of that company. Later he told me his income was half million a year. That was a shit load of money in those days.

3

When Angel came to the club to see me, we would sit at the corner table and have drinks with me. We talked about anything and always had a good laugh. When I had to do my dance routine he would sit at the table and tease me with 'dancing- dollars' so I would come up close and teased him. He was in love with my long legs and always wanted to touch them but didn't as he knew he wasn't allowed. He was just mucking around. When he got too close, I would raise my leg, and place a high-heeled foot on his shoulders and gently press down so he would back off. Occasionally he wanted a private show with me. Of course, the drinks would keep coming. As a dancer we had drinks for free at the club so I would sneak him my free drinks.

Angel loved watching me dance for him. After a couple months of knowing him, he asked me if I would go out with him sometime. I said, "Nar... you've got the wrong girl. You probably think you can just take me out and then have sex with me. No thanks."
He replied in his gentle voice, "I don't want to take you out for sex. All I want is your company."
I told him that I must work six days a week and I will lose money if I don't work.
He said, "However much you make a night I will pay you the same amount. No strings attached" I thought he was bullshitting and said I earn $500 a night. He agreed.

Golden years with my guardian Angel

He took me for dinner at a five-star restaurant. Then we went to a nightclub for more drinks. We had great fun that night. Angel could not dance for shit. We agreed that when I am on a dance floor he gets off because he is embarrassed. And when he wanted to dance, I would leave the floor. Can you imagine a businessman in an expensive suit and shoes behaving like a child when on a dance floor? He was having fun. Sometimes we did dance togeth-

PART THREE – THE WILD YEARS

er just to clown around. Then we would go and play the poker machines. He would give me the money to play with, and whatever I won he let me keep.

We became very close friends, no sex involved. I was still working as a dancer but cut it back to two or three nights a week. The other nights and days I was with him. He treated me with respect, kindness, no judgement, and most of all he adored me. Then one day My Angel proposed a deal. That I give up the dancing job and be his girl. He would pay me $2000 per week, plus he would rent a flat that I would live in, and he would visit when he did not want to go home to his wife. Yes, that was a lot of money. I agree to this deal on one condition that no sex was involved unless it was on my terms. Angel was an alcoholic and gambler, and all he wanted was to have a drinking partner. He did not care for sex!

I stopped working as an exotic dancer because I looked after My Angel, but he looked after me as well. That's why I think of them as the 'golden years'.

Every night we had great fun, going to nightclubs, restaurants, and sometimes a strip clubs. He would give me money that I would give to the girls who danced on a podium. I enjoy teasing the girls with the money, to come closer, and have a bit of flirtatious conversation. My Angel would sit in a corner of the club and watch from a distance. He used to love watching me doing those fun things. The drunker we became the more fun we had. When we partied hard, and he was too drunk to go home, he would come to my place and sleep on the couch until he sobered up and could drive back home.

That man could not even hurt a fly. He saved me so many times financially and emotionally. If I was in trouble, which as you now gather, happened often, he was always there for me.

I used to travel with him on his business trips. He wanted my company, someone to laugh and to drink with when his meetings were over. When he was in a business meeting I would either wait in the hotel room for him or go shopping. He always made sure that I was happy so he would leave his credit card. I could go and spend as much money as I wanted on shoes, bags, and expensive clothing. When he returned, I would show him what I purchased, sometimes I bought nice lingerie just for him. He loved it when I danced for him. He was a true gentleman. He was just happy to have someone with him and make him feel young again, and of course, to get away from his nagging wife. He used to call her the Gestapo. I was his getaway. After two years of partying hard together I felt comfortable and safe with him and became attracted to him. Then we became sexually intimate. He never asked me for sex. It was on my terms, when I wanted it. At that time, we had three agreements – that we would not fall in love with each other – that when I'm ready to make my own family he will let me go – and, I would never meet his wife. I told him, "If your wife finds out about us, not through me of course, and if she were to confront me about it, I would simply tell her I'm sorry, but I have not made your husband do anything that he did not want to do. This matter is between you and your husband."

Dangerous games

Luckily that never happened. She never knew about me. It was not so easy to not fall in love with each other. It started off with the sex, then we started making love – a big difference. We stopped straight away because we both realised we were falling in love.

There was one event, it was quite funny and sad at the same time. As usual we went out to have drinks, play pokies and do a bit of dancing. My Angel decided to go home but I was stubborn, I wanted to stay and drink more. Somehow, he convinced me to go. We left the club and on the way home there was a round fountain. When drunk, I get loud and very very cheeky. Standing next to the fountain, Angel wanted to tell me something. Out of nowhere I

PART THREE – THE WILD YEARS

pushed him into the fountain, in his beautiful expensive suit. Remember, he must go back to his wife... Well at 2 o'clock in the morning he is saturated from top to bottom. So, what were to do about his beautiful expensive suit? Me being drunk, and not thinking clearly, I put it in the dryer. Bad idea! It shrunk, and distorted, totally destroyed. Angel had to go back home and lucky for him his wife was sound asleep and so he could sneak in without her noticing that he was almost naked.

There were business meetings, often over lunch in a five-star restaurant. Those meetings usually involved signing contracts or to convince the client to come to his side, basically changing companies. My Angel often called me and instructed, "Dress to kill."

At these lunch meetings, everyone has a few drinks and relaxes. The client is not so uptight. The reason why he wanted me to be there, well the one obvious reason, I was his drinking buddy. But I was also there for distraction and entertainment, a bit of laughter, jokes, and me to be cheeky.

Those meetings were fun for all. When the meetings were finished, we would continue drinking and partying on baby!...

Stay away from my plate

As usual My Angel called me and asked me to come to dinner with him and his mates in a top restaurant. I asked him if I could bring along my friend Olga.
"Yes sure, why not".

Whenever I went to a restaurant with Olga, she never ordered anything. She would just pick from my plate. I hated that. It always happened.
I told her, "This being a five-star restaurant, you mustn't pick food off my plate... order something for yourself."

3

"No No. I won't pick any food off your plate".

We get to the restaurant all dressed up and looking pretty damn fine. Angel was already sitting at the table with his mates. We sat down at the table. The waiter soon came and asked us if we wanted a drink?
"Yes please."
Then later the waiter comes again, "Are you ready to order your meal?"
"Yes, we are."
"Olga, what would you like to order?"
As usual she did not want to order anything.
"You sure you do not want anything to eat? I don't want you to pick from my plate! I'm not fucking with you this time."
"No, it's okay... I am fine... thanks. I just want a few drinks".

We were having a nice time, a couple drinks, happily chatting between friends. Then the food arrives. It is beautifully served on lovely plates. We started eating and enjoying our food. Olga, sitting next to me, started looking at my plate like a hungry puppy.
"I wouldn't do it Olga if I were you! I'm asking you for the last time, do you want me to order you something?"
"No", then she immediately reached for my plate with her fork in her hand. With my fork already in my hand I stabbed her – not hard enough to damage but hard enough to make my point.
"Ouch!"
"I told you not to pick food from my plate."
Angel and his friends were horrified. Then they realised that Olga's hand was not bleeding. Nor did she complain. In fact, she was laughing then we all started laughing.
My Angel chuckled as he said to Olga, "She did warn you".
That girl never picked food from my plate ever again.

My Angel was always with me, wherever I went, whatever I was doing he knew. Not because he was a stalker or obsessed, we just totally trusted each other with everything. Till this day I keep his secrets and he keeps mine. Without judgement. He had the keys to our unit and came and went whenever he pleased. Fuck! Déjà vu! That just sounds like my mother… But with a big difference my angel was a gentleman and I certainly was not his whore.

Suit pants

Over the years, until this day he is still there for me. Even though I have stabbed him when I was drunk! Well not stabbed him. I tried to cut his pants suit because of something he did that pissed me off. When doing so I cut myself and blacked out. I woke the next day naked and covered in blood. Wondering what the hell did I do? I felt pain in my hand and saw the wound. I was worried and shitting myself because I could not remember what happened. I called my darling Angel, "What the hell happened last night?" "Don't worry darling… Nothing serious happened. You just cut my suit pants, and, in the process, you cut yourself". He continued, "You okay for tonight's partying and drinking?!"
My answer was, "Fuck yeah!"
"But darling," he giggled, "please don't push me in the fountain tonight… or cut my suit… it's too difficult." He was used to how crazy and cheeky I was. He loved that about me.

Moment of truth

One day My Angel rang me and asked me to meet him at a strip club. I said to him over the phone, I'm with my doctor now… I've got good news for you… I'll tell you when I see you.

I am an alcoholic and fight this disease every day. At that time, I knew I was an alcoholic so was at my doctor for a medicine to help me stop drinking, or should I say, it takes the desire off drinking. I was excited and looking forward to seeing him to let him

know about this positive step. When I arrived at the club he was with friends and drinking already. I came up to him from behind and covered his eyes. Boom! It's me darling. After I sat down and settled, I said, "Guess what?"
"What?"
"I went to the doctors and arranged for medicine that takes the desire of wanting to drink."
His face turned ghostly white.
I couldn't understand why he reacted as he did. I was hoping that he would be happy for me. Then he told me with his cute, sad face, "So who am I gonna drink with now?" I reminded him that I am still the same crazy and cheeky bitch and we will still party for as long as he wants.

The day was young, only 2:00 PM, there were hours for him to drink. Me without a drink! As I said before, I love to dance. We left the strip club for another nightclub. Because I was on this medication I did not want to drink, even though there was alcohol all around me. But I could not get on the dance floor because I was so nervous and insecure. I had a Red Bull hoping that would give me a bit of confidence. One Red Bull wasn't enough, two Red Bulls wasn't enough. I was really itching to get on the dance floor. All up I probably drank about thirty red Bulls. Finally, I had enough courage to dance. But hell, I was shaking and trembling, and my heart was pumping like it was about to explode. Another bad fucking idea!

The next day I told My Angel, "Fuck that! I'm not going to take this medicine, because I cannot get on a dance floor... I do not want to have to have thirty Red Bulls, with a heart that wants to explode."
Hearing this, Angel, with a smile from ear to ear, said, "I got my baby back! Let's party like we always do and forget all the stupid assholes".

We were two alcoholics, the only difference was he was in denial, I wasn't. I never judged him for that. He had his demons and I had mine.

Don't judge

You probably think, how could this man be an angel if all he does is drink and get me drunk. He never put a gun to my head to make me drink, that was my decision. He was an angel though. If I was in trouble, he would be there for me, no matter what. If I was struggling with money he would pay my bills, if I was sick, he would be at my side. We became so close that he called me his love child. When he used those two words, 'love child', I could feel it came from his heart. Don't get me wrong we had love, but our love was of two really close friends. We were committed to each other, trusted each other implicitly, and supported each other.

At the beginning of our time together, we made a pact that one day he must let me go for me to build my own family. I was twenty-seven. My Angel understood that. He would not leave his wife for me, and I would not ask him to do so.

Meet Peter

My Angel took his family away for a three-month holiday. I was bored without him and was not going to sit at home on my own. One night I went to a nightclub with a few friends. There, I met this short, fat, and bald man at the bar. His name was Peter. He lacked charm, was not good-looking, and was not very smart, but he did have a good sense of humour. We chatted about some silly show that seemed funny at the time. He made me laugh, and that's what attracted me to him. That he could make me laugh and not make me feel like a piece of meat that he just wanted to screw. After chatting for a long time, I decided to ask him to come home with me. Obviously, I had naughty thoughts in my mind. Of course, he said, "Yes".

Fortunately, this nightclub was just around the corner from where I lived. When we got to my place, I realised that was not my style. I was nervous. I asked him if I could have a couple cones. "Yeah, go for it", he said.

I had the cones but still could not bring myself to sleep with him so I asked him, "Could we go out and have a few more drinks? I am not drunk enough to have sex with you. He chuckled before saying, "We don't have to do anything that you don't want to do."
These words made me feel more comfortable and at ease. Anyway, we went back to the club for more drinks.

The next day I woke up naked next to Peter. I was confused because I had blacked out. I asked him what happened last night. He explained that I had too much to drink and fell asleep. Apparently, on the way home there were some Aboriginal people who tried to stop him from taking me home. Often the Aboriginal people, with their kids, sat around the fountain. They were protecting me because from time to time I gave the little kids a couple bucks, or sometimes took them to a McDonald's and fed them. Plus, I was always friendly to them. They saw how drunk I could get.

They took it on to protect me. Peter continued and said, "The Aboriginal people came and tried to stop me. They thought I was going to do something bad to you. I explained to them that I am trying to take you home safely. They followed us to your apartment to make sure that you got home okay".

Anyway, getting back to the story, I was sitting on my bed looking at myself in the mirror in the built-in wardrobe. I was naked, and Peter was sitting behind me, only in his undies. I asked him what happened when we got home... Did we have sex? He had a little smirk on his face. "Well, first you asked me to get undressed. Then

PART THREE – THE WILD YEARS

you didn't want to, then you did. You couldn't make up your mind."
"Did we fuck or not?!"
With a smile he said, "Finally you decided you wanted sex, and so we did".

   While I was sitting on the bed, with Peter looking at me through the mirror, he said, "You're going to be the mother of my children?" I thought to myself, *yep! You'll be the father of my children*.

   When I was fourteen, I set myself five goals. Buy a car, buy an apartment, get married, have my own business, and have children at age twenty-seven – I was twenty-seven. I did buy myself a car. Well, My Angel gave me the money. He also helped me to buy my first apartment.

   Within two weeks I was pregnant with Peter's child. The next step would be getting married. But it went a different way. I liked Peter but I did know what sort of person he was. Nor did he know me. But we were both happy with the potential of our first child.

Red flags

   Soon after that I met Peter's father, Glenn. I was washing the dishes at Glenn's with him cooking next to me. I said to Glenn, I'm glad I found the right man to be the father of my child.
   He replied in his sarcastic and quiet voice, "You sure about that?"
The way he said it alarmed me. Why would a father speak as such of his own son? Unless...

   I moved in with Peter at his parent's house. Peter's parents lived outside a country town, without public transport. The shopping centre was an hour away. Peter did not have a car and so used mine when he had to go somewhere.

3

When he used my car, and there was no one else at home I felt like a prisoner. That meant that I was stuck on a seven-acre property with no soul around me. The closest neighbour was at least two kms away.

Peter's real character came out. He became violent and abusive. One night I told Peter about a movie I had seen and how two lesbian chicks got away with $2 million from the mob. I told Peter I liked this movie because it's about two women kicking men's asses. Peter's reply was a hard punch to my face with his close fists. I thought my head would fall off my neck. The next day I woke up with a big purple bruise on my eye.

I quickly got dressed. I pulled my hair over my face while I walked outside. Glenn was in the kitchen and saw me running out of the door with my hair over my face. He made a comment, "It's starting already?"

I knew then and there that Peter was not the right man to be a father to my child to be. But it was too late. I was three months pregnant. I knew I had to escape from this man. I had nowhere to run and had no car to get away in.

Again, My Angel to the rescue

As usual My Angel was always there for me. I asked him if he could buy a cheap car for Peter, so when he is away, I can pack my stuff in my car and get out. This happened. When one morning Peter went somewhere I quickly packed and headed out.

While I was driving towards town, it happened that he was returning and saw me driving in the opposite direction. He turned his car around to follow me. My car was a sports car and so I accelerated. That shitty car of his was never going to catch me.

PART THREE – THE WILD YEARS

I went back to my apartment and changed the locks. As usual, My Angel was there for me through my pregnancy. We had not been sexually involved for a long time and now he became a father figure. The father that I should have had.

Premonition

Over the phone I told Peter to stay away from me otherwise I would put an affidavit on him. However, I did tell him that as the father of our child he would be welcome to visit her when she is born. I was not going to be that bitch that kept the father away from his child.

At six months pregnant, I had a horrible feeling and vision concerning Peter. I had to call him and warn him of what I saw. He did not answer his phone and so I left a message where I said, "Someone is going to die around you... it's something to do with drugs. I am only letting you know this because you are the father of my child."

Three more months passed, and it was time for me to give birth to my daughter Lee. She was born on a Saturday. I texted Peter to let him know that his child had been born. No reply. I called several times, no answer. It did not concern me that he did not respond as I presumed, he didn't want anything to do with the baby.

When Lee was born, I became depressed with baby blues. I was scared to touch her, feed her, bath her or change her nappies. On Monday Peter showed up. I was very much surprised, and a bit confused as to why he did not come earlier. He confessed that on weekends he goes to jail.
"What for?" I asked him.
"Fraud and stealing".
"Oh nice... Why didn't you reply to my messages?"
"I was in prison and that night my cellmate overdosed on heroin. But I

am here now."

I told Peter that our past is past and now we've got a little girl to look after. It's up to us to make it right for this innocent child.

I see you mummy!

Sometimes I see things before they happen, like Peter's warning regarding somebody's death. Usually, in my dreams I see what is going to happen. Sometimes I get visions. But this particular dream stuck in my head. In the dream I was sleeping on my bed in the lounge room. I preferred to sleep there as the view was much better. I could see the ocean and boats in the water as well as the beautiful horizon buildings surrounding the water. In the dream, or not in the dream, I do not know, I woke up and I saw a little girl, aged four or five years old. She was standing at the end of my bed and looking at me, right in my eye. She pointed her finger at me, waving her finger from left to right as a sign as if I am doing something wrong. The way she looked at me affected me because she looked like she was warning me and shaming me at the same time. I knew this was a premonition and warning. But for what?

PART THREE – THE WILD YEARS

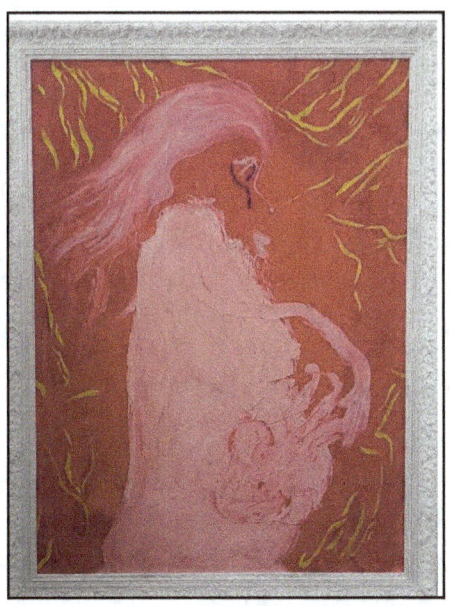

Love misunderstood
The struggle between a mother and teenage child.
The love is so strong, to protect the child from the life
unknown, and their own issues of discovery and rebellion.
This causes friction and pain for the mother as she tries
to protect her young with all her power.

Honey I am back

Peter and I decided to give it another go for the sake of this child. We purchased a house. The first months were fine. We took turns to attend Lee – feeding her, burping her and changing her nappies. Peter was excited and happy with his new daughter and was wonderful at that time.

There was one thing that my mother taught me, "Don't have sex for three months after a birth". And that stuck with me. After having Lee, I waited three months and guess what happened? I was

3

breastfeeding, I was on a pill, but still became pregnant. I call her my miracle child. At first, I thought, *holy shit, I'm pregnant again*. Peter was over the moon.

From the first moment of knowing that I was pregnant I started panicking again. Fortunately, that pregnancy was much easier. The moment Susanna was born I looked at her and I knew in my heart that she was the one who came to me in that dream. As she grew to the age four and five, she looked exactly like that girl from the dream – she was that girl. Now Susanna is a grown woman, and she has the gift as well. She can see things before they happen, and she can communicate with the other side. Now, that shit is freaky.

I know in my heart that Suzanne is an old soul as well. I believe and I feel in my heart that in our past lives we knew each other and always found a way back to each other. That's why she came to me in my dream before she was born to warn me and to look at my life, to take better care of myself – before she would find a way back to me in this life.

When Susanna was born Peter reverted to his controlling behaviour. He was verbally and physically abusive. We were struggling for money. Even though we had our own business, money was a big problem. Peter had the image in his head of the perfect family – trophy wife, house, and children, whilst ignoring and being in denial of our financial problems. He was obsessed with racing pigeons and had thousands of them. His pigeons came first, before me or his children. The business at that time was a chicken farm. I was the bookkeeper. It was hard work and made no profit. We struggled for food and battled to pay the mortgage. I kept telling Peter that the chicken farm is costing us money as there is no profit in it. My pleas fell on deaf ears. We were falling further behind with the rent for the chicken farm ($8000 every eight weeks), as well as the water and electricity bills. But Peter was constantly on the phone bitching about his pigeons with one person or another.

The monthly home phone was $3000 per month, a fortune in those days, even now. So much money owed.

There was little money for food or for our children's needs. My Angel was still around and when I was extra tired, or depressed, he would come and help me with the children. He would change nappies and feed them. It was not fair for me to ask for financial help, so I kept my mouth shut. You probably wonder how My Angel was still around if I was in the relationship. I told Peter that My Angel was my father figure. And he will always be in my life and when we get married, he's the one who is going to walk me down the aisle. Peter had no objection to it, whatsoever.

Desperate to meet another angel

At this stage of my life I had little booze or drugs. I stopped when I first fell pregnant and was clean for my children – to be a homemaker, and not a homewrecker.

When it got to that stage of us being so desperate for money, I put an advert in the newspaper for a 'sugar daddy', hoping to find someone who would like my company and my friendship without sexual relationship. I must have been dreaming!

I had many phone calls from men and set coffee-dates with five-men. I explained to them what I was looking for. None were interested once they heard there were no sex benefits and I was dejected and exhausted. The last gentleman that I met offered to buy groceries in exchange for sex. I was desperate so I agreed. First, we went to the shops and bought the groceries, which he put in his car. I followed him to a hotel to complete the deal. Only then did he give me the groceries.

This agreement was against my morals, but what could I do? I was hungry, my children were hungry, and Peter lived in his dream-

3

world.

I was disgusted with myself but when the kids saw the shopping and started picking out their favourite food, their big smiles made me feel less bad about myself. There were so many bags on the floor, and the cost was $800. Peter did not ask where I got the money for the groceries.

I was pleased the children were happy but the shame and the guilt would not leave me. I could not live with the knowledge that I had swapped my body for groceries. A couple weeks later I told Peter. As usual he was in denial and said that I'm lying. It's like he didn't care. Everything is fine in his mind, or he did not want to acknowledge that I was forced to do what I did.

The pigeons always came first. When he arrived from the farmyard, he would come through the front door and head straight out the back door to his pigeons. He didn't even acknowledge me or say hello to the children. There was a lot of work cleaning them, feeding them, training them, and applying medicine to the sick ones. Some of the pigeons were born deformed or there was something wrong with them, so he would break their necks. He did this without feeling or emotion.

In terms of people, he judged everyone, "They're fucking junkies", or "lowlife's", "morons" and "fucking idiots". That was his way of looking at the world. I didn't see it back then but now I see it, clear. Add to this his game of playing emotional abuse, physical abuse, sexual abuse, which included rape! I tolerated it all for the kids.

Since Lee was born (four years), our sex life has never been great. I call him the Eight Seconds Man, more like Four Second Man. Daily abuse turned sex into rape. We had a double story house. The bottom floor was a granny flat. Things got so bad between us that I slept in the granny flat. I had baby monitors with me so I could hear the children upstairs. I would lock myself in but when he wanted sex there was no stopping him. He would bang on the door like a demented child to get in. I had two choices. Don't let him in and try and put up with an hour or more of banging, which would eventually wake up the children. Or I could open the door and let him have his way (besides, it would only last four seconds anyway). I chose the four second.

I would just lay there and cry, while he had his way with me, whilst he would tell me, "You know why I love you? Because you are so stupid".

I finally decided to leave Peter. Once again it was not easy to get away from him. But My Angel was always there for me. Peter knew how much the children meant to me. He would never let me go with them. I asked My Angel if he could rent an apartment for me, one that is close to my children. Of course, he did. The apartment was only ten minutes away from them. I could come and go when I wanted to see them. That came with a price though, as I had to give myself to Peter.

Peter convinced me one more time to come back to him. And the great weapon that he had against me were the children. I returned. Another bad idea.

*Together the darkness has no power of the light.
No matter how lonely you are or that you believe you stand alone, there always will be someone to help you. Someone who could be in your life without you even knowing it. It could be a stranger, an acquaintance, a friend, family, or even someone or something that you cannot see like your guardian angel. Even you may not believe that there is someone watching over you. Still if you just let someone give you a hand or even be brave enough to ask for help, then you can overcome any obstacle, where together you reach the light. There is the well-known saying 'There is a light at the end of the tunnel'.*

Run! Again run...

Peter became much more violent, emotionally, and mentally abusive. I did not know what to do. I knew I could not continue like this. Worse though, the children were experiencing this type of relationship and growing up thinking *it's okay for a man to hit a woman*.

Again I decided to completely get away from him. I found a women's refuge, where they were willing to take me and the kids. We escaped when he was at the farm.

PART THREE — THE WILD YEARS

When leaving Peter for this refuge, I was completely bankrupt, so I filed for bankruptcy. Yes, my Angel helped me buy my first unit before I met Peter. When I decided to partner with Peter, I sold the unit to help buy a family home for the four of us. Peter was broke when I met him. Everything was in my name: the bill's, mortgage, and the rented farm. But I didn't care because I was free of this financial burden. I was free of him. Peter remained in his denial dream, until he had a wake-up call when the bank took the house. He was forced to move out.

When I was in the refuge, I had to go back to the house to get some stuff for the kids. I went with the children. That was just before he received the news about the bank taking the house. He pinned me to the couch and forced himself on to me, raping me in front of our children. Once he had finished his business, I quickly grab what I could and left as fast as possible. I just hope that the kids were too little to remember.

Back to shit

At the women's refuge I learnt that I am not the only one in that situation. I was there for three months. It was the staff from the refuge who helped me find a house through the Housing Commission. This was in The Western Suburbs of Sydney. The worst suburb that you could live in. It was full of junkies, filth, and lots of violence. I was so depressed that I started drinking again.

On weekends Peter had the children, that was when I abused the drugs and booze. I, over a period, started drinking more every day. I just wanted the voices in my head to stop! The voices that said, *You are not good enough, you are a fuck up, look at the bad job you are doing with the children.* I felt so much shame.

3
Oh, Jackie boy

I got myself involved with the next door neighbour, Jack. Of course, anyone I seemed to get involved in had demons. Jack had plenty. He was big, strong, athletic, and schizophrenic. The schizophrenia was aggravated by being on hard-core drugs and booze. When on the drugs he was scary and badly paranoid. He could so easily pick me up and throw me up in the air like I was a piece of paper. I knew that was a bad romance, but there was something about him that attracted me to him. I almost fell in love with him.

My Angel would come and visit from time to time and help me as well. When he came, Jack and his family would see Angel's car in front of my house. Jack's family was huge, all living in that one house, like hillbillies. As soon as they got their dole, they would blow it on alcohol and drugs. They were trash, and almost every night would binge throughout the night. The cops were always there to stop fights and violence.

One night, I went to their party. Everything was going okay until the moment they mentioned My Angel. I told them that I was not sexually involved with him, and he is like a father figure for me. They did not care to believe me and argued with me about it. This was tiring and I had had enough and said loudly to my girlfriend (who came with me), "Let's go, we don't need this shit!". The hillbillies got pissed off.

Soon as we left the house, all of them, and I mean at least fifteen people followed us and jumped us. I couldn't see where my friend was because I was being bashed. Somehow Jack got me free and told me to run home. When I got home my friend was already there. She was bruised and scratched. The next morning we looked at each other and saw the damage they had done to us – our bodies felt like we had been hit by a truck – black eyes, swollen lips. I had a broken rib. I couldn't move, I couldn't speak, and I could not breathe properly, because it hurt like crazy.

PART THREE – THE WILD YEARS

My stalkers

After that, Jack and I saw each other in secret. But still, his family stalked me, harassing me in public, harassing me at home and they even scratched my car with the word 'whore'. I was scared at nights in my own home and the safety of my children. I could not go to the police, because if I did, they would have been even worse to me when the police left.

But this time I did not have much support from the government or the Department of Housing. I was stuck living in that house and so headed back to the woman's refuge.

Those people that run the show in the Department of Housing did not take my complaint seriously. I offered them a thick folder of pictures of the property damage the stalkers did, of my bruised and battered body from their physical abuse. I Also had copies of their threatening letters addressed to me. Their reason was because I wouldn't to go to the police and report them, for obvious reasons. Therefore, for not having an affidavit on them the Department could not help me. Just another bureaucratic bullshit. Not enough paperwork for them to prove that I and my children were in danger.

I had to find somewhere to live for the girls. I found the cheapest apartment I could afford while I was on the list for another house from the Department.

Breakdown

After all of this, I had a major breakdown. I was drinking heavily and smoking marijuana. Depression, booze, and grass are not good companions. I was cracking up. Peter took advantage of this, using all of this to turn the children against me. Thank God they were too little to understand. He was still having the children on weekends and because of my breakdown I let him look after them for longer periods. I did not have the strength to carry on. I knew they would be okay with their father whilst I tried to get my shit together. Then I would fight for my children.

I took myself off to the mental unit hospital as I had suicidal intent. The latest event in a list of events was that Peter told me that I will never see Lee or Susanna again. When I went into the hospital, I took a razor with me to cut my veins. I couldn't imagine life without my children. In the state I was in I was not thinking straight.

When in my room in the hospital, out came the razor, and I started to cut my veins. The razor was blunt, and it was painful. I went to the nurse and asked for a razor, telling her that I needed to shave my legs. And mind you, I was admitted that same day with suicide thoughts. Not only that, but my record also probably showed that I took those sleeping tablets to end my life when my mother booted me out. And that stupid dummy gives me one as she asks me, "Are you suicidal?"
"Me no. Of course not." I am just bit fucked up but that's okay I'll be fine thinking to myself. What a stupid moron she was.

Back in my room I immediately started hacking into my veins. Jackpot, I hit the main artery. I put pressure on the artery to encourage faster bleeding. It seemed to take forever, and was hurting like mad. When I looked around, blood was all over the bed and carpet, and I sort of got mesmerised. Then I thought of the children without me. I left the room with my arm dripping blood and made my way to the nurse's counter. She was shocked when she saw me, especially my room. After that I do not remember clearly what happened.

Later, the nurse that looked after me was kind. She could not believe that I was given a razor on the very day I was admitted. That first nurse got into lots of trouble for giving me the razor.

I did not want my children to see me in that state, so I pushed myself away from them, not calling or seeing them. It was too painful, and I hoped that by not seeing them or talking to them I could get myself together, faster. That separation tore me apart.

When discharged from the mental hospital, I placed myself in rehab for alcohol and marijuana abuse. I was determined to get clean. I was in rehab for three weeks. When I got out, I tried to get my children back without a big fight in the courts. I organised mediation between me and the father. I wanted to have shared custody of our children. I didn't want to be a bitch and stop him from seeing them, or not to give him a chance to do the right thing by our children. But he didn't show up and ignored the process. I tried to reason with him, and I thought that he would behave like a grown-up, especially when it came to his children. But he would have none of it.

As I was preparing myself for the court, I had a supervised urine test to prove I was drug free. I also completed a parenting certificate so I could be seen as competent.

I gained a lawyer through Legal aid, so it was free. She was understanding and helpful. I told her of my cleaning up and what I had done in preparation. She said I had done all the right things.

When it came to the court day Peter showed up with his lawyer. My lawyer went to talk privately to his lawyer before the case was due. She returned with a giggle and smile on her face. She told me, "He doesn't believe the urine test was real, so he wants my blood sample." I laughed and replied, "That's fine... but I want his blood sample."

She went back to his lawyer and advised that I am willing to have another blood test but only if he is tested. I believe at that time he was on speed. His answer was no, and they accepted the results of my urine test.

Because I had done all the right things and prepared myself for that court day, the judge placed the children in my care until the next hearing, which was in two weeks' time. I was delighted.

In the meantime, Peter called me before the court day and asked me, "How far am I willing to go to get the children?" He even tried using my psychiatrist against me by trying to get them to write him a letter regarding my mental health. Of course, that costs money, which he didn't have. I said to him, "I'll fight you till the day I die".

He relented and said, "Okay, have it your way. I'm not gonna fight you in court. You can have the children." Because he was mean to me and used my children against me, I decided to go full custody for my children. With access for him on weekends to see them.

When we returned to court on the due date, we already had come to agreement between us. Peter didn't put up much of a fight and thank Jesus for that.

I was relieved and happy to get my children back.

Honey I'm home

Practical jokes. Yes, I love them. Pigeon man!... The father of my children. The short, fat, and bald one, who if green would be the twin of Schreck.
Peter has moved on and got married. Yay!! Anyway, one day, my daughters and I decided to play a practical joke on him. But first there are rules for practical jokes. Such as, do not hurt the victim, nor destroy their property. That's what I told my daughters, Lee, and Susanna. My girls told me that their father leaves the window open a crack at the back of the house when he goes out. Hmm?! Let's play a practical joke on your father.
The girls were excited and asked, "What should we do?"

PART THREE – THE WILD YEARS

I had it, just the right idea – to scare the shit out of him and his new wife.

I went to the butcher's and asked for blood, lots of blood. Yes, you heard me right, blood. The blood was watery and not thick enough to look like human blood. The butcher asked me why I wanted so much blood. I told him, my girls and I are gonna play a practical joke on their father. He looked at me in a funny way but gave me advice as to how to make the blood thicker. "Go to the shops and get corn starch. Mix this with the blood." He also said it would be easy to wipe off when the joke is over. I took his advice. When I got home, I mixed cornstarch with the blood, and it became nice and thick.

The plan was to go to Peter's place when he and the wife were at work and splatter the blood on the floor and walls to make them think there must have been a murder, or a ghost in their house.

The girls knew the time when neither would be home. The clever little monkeys were only around seven and eight years old then. We got to Peter's house and as hoped, no one was there. The girls took me around the back of the house and Lee climbed through the narrow window opening. She unlocked the door from the inside.

The girls were so excited and wanted to put the blood everywhere. We decided to make blood tracks on the kitchen floor. As well as some blood on an old broken TV. To make things scarier, we put blood on their wedding photo frame.

I advised the girls not to touch anything else or take anything. We went home to wait for his reaction. Unfortunately, one of the girls could not help herself and took her earphones back to my place. This was a dead giveaway. Luckily, Peter did not notice the earphones, at first. Later he did and then knew it was us in his house. But not before they freaked out. Apparently, when they came home that day and saw the blood everywhere, Peter's wife totally snapped.

3

I was itching to know what went through their heads when he found their home like that. Later, I called Peter on a pretence and asked when he was to collect the girls for the weekend. I made no mention about blood.
Peter asked, "Were you in my house?"
I said No and pretended I did not know what he was talking about. "I know you were here with the girls because a set of earphones are missing".
I couldn't help myself and laughed and told the truth.

Funny enough, Peter wasn't angry. In fact, he was impressed, "You scared the living shit out of my wife. We had to go to a hotel that night."
The girls could hear because I had him on loudspeaker, and they burst out laughing. "She", his wife, "made me put deadlocks on all of the doors. She was so scared she wanted to see a psychic, to see who was dead. Especially when she found our photos with the blood on it." Peter heard us three laughing and he could not believe that the girls had kept their mouth shut and didn't say anything. Well, when it comes to practical jokes my girls are good.

More jokes

When you play a practical joke on someone, expect them to return in kind. That's the whole point. If you can give, you must be able to take it in return.

From time to time my friend Nicole would come to my place to babysit my daughters.
On one visit to Nicole's place, we had a few drinks, whilst the girls were occupied with computer games. After a couple drinks, obviously you need to go to the toilet, right? I went to do my business. Suddenly Nicole frantically calls, "Anna! Anna! Come quick!"
I stick my head outside the toilet door to see what's happening. I

could see the room they were in. And I could see the bed end and at the edge of the bed Lee was leaning over while Nicole was holding her head, at the same time, screaming, "She's bleeding. She hit her head on the bed". I freaked seeing all the blood. But I saw a tiny smirk on Lee's face and realised that they are fucking with me. They used tomato sauce to pretend it was blood. Oh my God what have I done? I have turned my daughters into little monsters.

Payback time

I, Lee, and Suzanne were with Nicole. Lee was nine, Suzanne was eight. We decided to play a practical joke on Nicole. We were at the petrol station close to a Woolworths. I needed petrol for my car. I asked Nicole if she could go next door to Woolworths and get bread, while I filled up with petrol. Lee and Susanna were in the car. I got out of the car and started putting in the petrol. When Nicole was gone, I told the girls to get into the boot and stay quiet. It was safe as they could enter the boot from inside the car and so there was fresh air. "We are going to play a practical joke on Nicole, but you must stay quiet in the boot till I tell you to come out."

I finished putting the petrol in and I saw Nicole making her way back to the car. Before she got into the car I asked with pretended concern, "Where are the girls?"
Nicole looked horrified, "I thought they were with you".
"No, they said they wanted to go with you. I said yes, so they followed you and were right behind you when I saw them last."
Nicole starts shaking and panicking. Quickly she said, "I'll run back to Woolworths and look for them".
"No!" I said, "get into the car! We'll drive around and look for them." By that time Nicole was totally in shock and full of fear. Once she got into the car I started laughing. Nicole looked at me with her face covered with tears. Then I say, "Okay girls come out." They crawled out of the boot through the back seat opening. We

all start laughing. At first poor Nicole just looked at me and then laughed with us. "You bitch. I'm gonna get you for that". Oh well, at least she took it well. But what she had in store for me was genius.

Art Gallery invitation

I am an artist and work with oil paintings on canvas. Art is my passion, that's how I express my feelings. The images in this book are mine. I'm not a well-known artist, yet. As a new artist to the industry, it is difficult to get my name out. I have been to many galleries to show my work, but most gave me the cold shoulder. I guess my art is too raw for some people.

Nicole's father worked for some big-shot company, and he got tickets for an exhibition at a well-known art gallery. So I thought. Unfortunately, he could not attend the event. Nicole asked me if I wanted a ticket to go. I was excited at the prospect as perhaps I may meet people who can help me promote my art. I asked Nicole if she would come with me? "No! art galleries are not my scene".

A few days later I received an email from the gallery to confirm my invitation. I thought to myself, finally I may find someone who will take interest in my art. And dreaming big, maybe even have my art displayed in their Gallery.

The event was still two weeks away. In that case what do I need? I need a new dress, new shoes, have my hair and nails done, and all the time Nicole was encouraging me, "Yes, a new dress, new shoes…"

I told Nicole that I received the email confirmation of my invitation. I expressed my gratitude for this opportunity to express my love for art. I spent hours telling her of my hopes to 'be discovered'.

The night before the events I went to Nicole's, full of excitement, and again told her how much I appreciate the ticket. I did this while I painted my toenails. That was when Nicole burst out laughing.
"It's a joke" she said.
What? What do you mean a joke... what joke?
"There is no such gallery opening. I tricked you".
I did not believe her at first. I did not want to believe her. I was confused.
"I made it all up," she said.
"What the fuck do you mean?"
"The tickets I gave you were made from clothing tags."
"No? It can't be. I received the email from them. It looked so real."
"I set up the email and I sent it to you".
"You bitch! I do not know if I should hate you or be angry at you?"

The way she set up this was brilliant and her acting deserves an Oscar. She had me going till the last moment. Lucky that she told me the night before, otherwise I would have been searching for a gallery that did not exist.

Never mind finding Memo! Finding dildo

Every woman has some sort of toy, for herself. A backup plan... ha ha. I had one when I was single. Not because I'm a sex maniac, quite the opposite. But I do like to flirt a bit in the cheeky way. There was a period of three years that I was not sexually active. Mentally, sex was just not on my mind. But a human body has its own natural needs and when you do not think about sex or even wanting it your body will let you know it's time to get 'serviced'.

Example: A scientific fact is that men wake up with a hard on, regularly. They are able to do something about it.
In my experience, when I have surreal dreams of having sex, that's my body's way of telling me it's time to release some hor-

3

mones. So, I went and bought myself a vibrator. I named it Mr Pinky, Man of the house. In fact, Mr Pinky was a perfect man; it didn't argue back, didn't give shit, stayed quiet until needed, I didn't need to cook for Mr Pinky.

Mr Pinky lived in my nightstand drawer, next to my bed. I thought it was a good place to hide it. So I thought...

When my girls were about six or seven years old they were playing in my room. Jumping on my bed. Then they decided to play dress-up in my clothes and hunted through my wardrobe. Going through my nightstand they find Mr Pinky. Oh my, I panicked. Shit! What do I do, how do I explain this without making a big deal about it? Children are curious and like to explore – full of questions.

I had two choices... Panic and quickly grab that vibrator from them and hide it somewhere else, and not talk about it. Or, the better choice, gently take it back from them without making a big deal of it. Which is what I did.
Then the questions started. "Mummy, what is this?"
"It's mummy's massager."
"Can we use it?"
"It's not working at the moment."
"Can you fix it?"
"It needs batteries but when I get the batteries then you can play with it" and I left it at that. Fortunately, they lost interest in Mr Pinky.

If I went with the first choice, quickly grabbing Mr Pinky from them it would just make them more curious. And probably, they would try to sneak into my bedroom to play with Mr Pinky, using it like some sort of fighting sword.

The shit that the kids came up with can be hilarious. You must be quick with your answers, without panic. The best way is to stay calm and explain to them. Sometimes it's good to tell them a white lie, because they are too little to understand fully.

My baby!

Besides my passion for music and art, I love animals, especially dogs. They don't talk back, and are loyal guard dogs if you're a good owner.

Peter found a stray, which he took to his place. He is not an animal lover unless they are pigeons. Well in that case good for me. The dog was too destructive for Peter, especially with his pigeons. Anyway, I took over the dog.

Because he found the dog on the street he gave it the name, Lucky. I changed the name to Lockita, which in Spanish means crazy woman. Just like its mummy.

When I got Lockita I kept her in the house. Each night when I watched TV Lockita would sleep next to me on the couch. For the first six months she had severe nightmares. In her sleep she would make weird noises and even cry.   I would gently stroke her and softly wake her up so she could snap out of the nightmare.

Lockita is my best friend and my personal bodyguard. One night she ran out of the house and onto the street. I did not realise this straightaway but when I did, I panicked. Suddenly I heard a loud bang. Running out as quickly as I could I saw the car speeding off leaving Lockita on the road.

I ran to her and I picked her up and tried to get her back in the house. She was only about twelve months old, but already too big and heavy for me to easily manage. But I did it. Then I could see how badly she was hurt. She was bleeding from her mouth and her jaw was broken. She was in great pain.   I panicked and cried

3

and had no idea what to do. I remember watching the movie, *K9*, where the detective runs with his dog to the hospital emergency.

I did not know at that time that there were animal hospitals, besides vets.

I called 000 for emergency. I ask them to send an ambulance, telling them that my baby was hit on the road. The operator tried to ask me questions. "Where is your baby now?" "How old is your baby?" I said she is twelve months old. The operator must have thought babies at that age usually crawl and start to walk. Then the operator asked, "Where did your baby get hit?"
"On the road!"
I could tell that she was confused and asked me to stay on the line until the ambulance arrived.

Finally, the ambulance arrived with a siren sounding and a screech of brakes. Two paramedics rushed in. When they saw me on the floor with the dog hysterically crying, "My baby got hit, please help!" Immediately, one of the guys ran out of the house so quickly you could almost see the smoke coming out of his ears.

When he came back in, he said to me, "I had to cancel the helicopter that was to come and pick up 'your baby' because it's a dog! Do you realise that you could receive a heavy fine for doing this! Do you know there is 'animal' hospital emergency?"
I said to him I had no idea what that was.

When they left I phoned an animal hospital and got the address. I got Lockita into my car and drove like crazy to get her there quickly. Finally, she was looked after properly, and her wounds attended to. They administered pain control and gave me painkillers to take home.

PART THREE — THE WILD YEARS

On the case

I was so pissed off with the driver that hit Lockita and ran away I was determined to find the bastard. The car was a silver sedan. Because the hit-and-run happened around five in the afternoon, I figured that this person probably was returning from work and lives in the area.

The next day was a weekend, so I drove around the suburb looking for the car hoping they were at home.

It occurred to me to use my spiritual powers to find the car. I took Lockita's collar with me. It was covered with blood. I held it firmly and started to calm myself down. I said my little prayer and asked for guidance to lead me to this car. I drove every street in my suburb, checking each driveway for a silver sedan car. As I drove, I tightly held Lockita's leash, whilst picturing her getting hit by that car. By my picturing this scenario I could visualise the impact of the car hitting my dog. I also imagined putting myself in that person's body, as if I was the one who was driving. Doing so allowed me to see what they saw through their eyes whilst driving. It doesn't always work, but most of the time, if I do it right, it works like a charm.

I found the car, and that prick had not even washed the blood off it. I wrote down the plate number, the make of the car, and the address. I called the animal hospital to let them know who hit my Lockita, and that I had proof as the blood is still on the car. All they had to do was to take a sample from the car and compare it to my dog's blood. But no, they couldn't be bothered. All they were interested in was could I afford to pay the bill, otherwise they would take my dog away from me. That just made my blood boil.

At first, I wanted to do voodoo to the hit and run driver, but I know that with karma, what you put out you get back in return, so I left it to the universe to take care of, better that way.

3

Happily, Lockita made a full recovery and spends hours on the couch, snuggled next to me. I also have a cat, but that is another story.

PART - FOUR Finishing up

I am an alcoholic

After all my misfortune and demons there is always the temptation of taking a sip from the Devils Cup – alcohol! I fight this disease every day.

I am on medication that helps me to stay away from alcohol. But unfortunately, this medicine now is out of stock. My biggest fear is to fall again. Each day I pray for strength to resist temptation and give me the strength to say no. I am not preaching to anyone, but this is the way I help myself.

My Art

Some describe my art as dark. My art is throughout this book, so you decide for yourself. Perhaps it is dark, but my paintings are very close to me and represent my feelings. A lot of people are afraid to express their emotions, I lay mine on canvas for the world to see.

I think my artistic opening was seeing my father creating large floral arrangements. On these he needed fancy writing on the dedication. As my handwriting was good and could be fancy, he got me to 'letter' the cards.

Ella (the nice one) was an interior designer, and so she had artistic talent. When she moved into our house, she redid the kitchen and I watched as she explained.

I did not do art at school because of my rebellion. I did not give a shit, so that didn't help. But I did easily design my own Communion dress as explained earlier.

I did not go to any art school. Not because I didn't want to, I just did not know if I had any talent. My painting just happened. One day on a whim, I went and purchased canvas and paint, and art appeared. After that, all I knew was that I wanted to paint more and more. I made a deal with myself that I would not paint whilst under the influence of alcohol or any other stimulant. I have kept that promise to myself. When painting, I'm sober, at the moment, alone. I usually play classical music. So when my daughters hear music from my art room, they know Mama is working.... and do not interrupt.

When my friends saw that first painting some said, "You should sell it as it is good". As I continued painting, they said, "You should have an exhibition". I decided to set up a website for my paintings and show the world I even design my website.(www.annamariaartist.com)

I have entered competitions, but my paintings are raw. Nor are they everyone's cup of tea, especially for those who are normal. Seeing my paintings makes them wonder, *What's going on in that woman's head?* But that's okay as that is the reaction I want. Good or bad, I want to show the world that in my work it's okay to share my pain, and that you are not alone.

What makes me tick?

I cannot handle people who look you in the eye and lie at the same time. It's like they're spitting in my face and then telling me it's raining. Don't get me wrong, everyone lies. The question though, is... are they lying for the wrong reasons or are they lying to protect their loved ones. And when someone is lying to me it feels like an insult to my intelligence.

As mentioned, I hate cooking. Don't get me wrong I'm a good cook, well that's what my children used to say, "Mummy you should be on the MasterChef". Now they say, "You can't cook for shit Mum." The reason why I do not like to cook is from hearing my father boast, "That women are only good for cooking and fucking." That sentence is stuck in my head. I'll never slave in the kitchen for a man. But when I choose to cook for someone special it's my way of showing my appreciation to the one that I love or respect. I put my heart and soul into cooking.

Mother

You may want to know about my current relationship with my mother. I thought I would never hear her cry or give her an apology. All I ever wanted from her was her love. Not long ago I called to check on her. She started crying on the phone and apologised for being a bad mother and not being there for me. I don't know what led her to say these things. I went quiet and had to pinch myself as she confessed to many shortfalls. She said that she had been a bad mother and was never there for me. Yet, I have mixed feelings about her sincerity. I am grateful though because it is a new beginning for us. I love this woman with all my heart. She is my mother after all. But that phone call was all manipulative.

She owns a two-story house. She lives on the ground floor, and my brother on the top floor. She's been well looked after by my brother who provides whatever she needs. So, when I go to visit my brother, I usually see her. She is the same as usual, often cold hearted, miserable, angry with life, and especially angry with me.

My Brother

That house I just mentioned was bought and paid off with funds

from my mother's mystery man Mario. My brother renovated it, and so lives on the first floor as he does not have to pay rent. My brother is married to a good lady, and they have two kids.
Now, after all these years, as a family we have a good relationship, and for the first time in my life I love some festival days, such as Christmas, birthdays, and Easter, when we have family get-togethers. The food is good, my kids will come – I love it.

Father

For half of my life I have been told by my father that I am stupid. Over and over again I grew up thinking that I was stupid. But I forgive him for all that he did to me. There was a time I went back to Poland to visit after ten years of being away. All I wanted was for my father to admit his abuse and apologise, and acknowledgement. As soon as I arrived, I wanted to talk with him, before he got drunk. I wanted to tell him how he made me feel and the fear that I had. When I tried to talk to him, he made excuses or had explanations. But for a single moment he went quiet and looked at the floor. His face was awash with remorse and sorrow. In that moment, I saw his regret, his pain. He was sorry. And yet, he could not say "Anna, I'm sorry". I could see it in his face, but he could not say it aloud. That was enough for me. That's when I forgave him for everything that he had done because I could see his own pain and regret in that moment. He still lives in Poland with his eighth wife or is it his ninth. I've lost my account. It's no longer a florist man but a real estate wheeler and dealer. By now he probably owns half the city. Even though he's got all that money he is still a bloody scrooge. He is well set up for the rest of his life, and good for him.

Spiritual beliefs – Gift or curse?

As mentioned, I have been blessed, or cursed, depends which

4

way you look at my spiritual gift. Some people would give a label such as schizophrenia, witchcraft, psychic, medium, clairvoyance blah blah blah.

I do not belong to any religion. I believe my mother has a Jewish background. When I asked her about her mother's maiden name, she would not tell me. My mother was born just after the Second World War, and so I can understand why she may want to hide it. I am spiritual, but not religious. I believe in treating others as I want to be treated, that is, with respect and compassion. When I pray, I use the words "Father Jesus". Yes, it might be confusing to some because Jesus is of all the Christian religions. For me though, I speak to Jesus, directly, not via a Christian religion. After all, he will talk to me that way.

When I talk to him, it's like meditating. I clear my mind of thoughts. Breathe deeply and exhale slowly. I talk to him in my mind just like I am talking to you now. I don't say any prayers that are written in any Bible. I basically have a conversation with him. Sometimes when I'm deep in "my prayers" I feel his presence. It's overwhelming to the point that I cry from happiness that I feel physically and emotionally. The tears are tears of joy. It is an unbelievable feeling when I'm connecting with him. It almost feels like an out of body experience. And I'm not a nutter.

I mainly believe in him, Mother Nature, Angels in spiritual and physical form. I believe strongly that we all have Angels and that they are around us all the time for guidance. I think they give us messages, but not always directly. They could be via your psychologist, your neighbour, your best friend, words from a book or even a stranger who walked past you and gave a nice greeting, and perhaps some other words. These always make my day and lift my spirits.

Sometimes I see things before they happen. They could be in a dream or while I am awake. I saw 911 in a dream a year before it

PART - FOUR Finishing up

happened: I saw buildings falling down with thick smoke covering the scene. I saw people running in panic. I did not know at that time it was a premonition but at the same time I could not get the image out of my head. Then one day I was on the phone and the TV was on in the background. As I glanced at the TV, I saw the news coverage. I watched in horror. It was exactly the same scene that I had in my dream. I broke down crying and fell on the floor. I could not get out of my head.

I believe we are all born with six senses, in addition to touch, smell, audio, sight and taste. Then puberty comes, and that's when your gift of the sixth sense either stays or diminishes. Lucky, I am not from past centuries, otherwise my ass would be toast.

Yes, I believe in heaven but with my past I doubt that it will let me in! As you know I have seen my own hell so what makes you think there is no heaven? I believe our biggest fear is our own hell. My biggest fear is to be alone. And that's what I saw in my hell – darkness and loneliness. I must be gentle on myself, knowing the loneliness of my early and later years.

My personal belief is that we have many lives. And each life given is different to the previous. You can be born into a life of privilege of wealth and health. And through that life your beliefs are tested. Tested in your faith, your kindness, your strength, your courage, and your grace. The next life might be a life of poverty, but still you'll be tested in your faith.

I have had glimpses of my past lives, where I remember things not of this life. I also have feelings or emotions that can only belong to another time. For example, when I'm watching a movie and there are kings or queens, I know the beautiful dresses, and how heavy they were. I do not remember who I was or what sort of life that I had, but I do remember the feeling of those dresses. I know this is my last life, and why not share it with you?

There is that wonderful book *Life After Life* (1975) by psychiatrist Raymond Moody, who interviewed and documented the cases of some 150 people who had stories of near-death experiences. These are fascinating. I am sure if he interviewed me, that we would both learn a lot about my past lives.

I have a special bond with fire. When relaxed, as I just spoke about, concentrating on my energy is positive and not controlling I can connect with fire. It's all about energy. I have to let the fire know that I'm not going to put it out. And when I light a candle and stare at the flame, after a while the flame will follow my finger or my hand. It's like dancing with the fire. When I show someone this trick, especially when I put my hands into the fire, they can't believe that I do not get burnt. Sitting by a fire I become hypnotised and mesmerised by its flames and power.

I do not know why I have this love affair with fire, perhaps something good happened around fire in a past life. I believe that in this current life, and in past lives, that I have used fire for cleansing and (good) spells, which remove bad energy.

Karma, I believe can be a bitch with the capital B. I try to do no harm to others because I do not want that bitch to come back to bite my ass. There are two sides to Karma though, the good and the bad. So why not focus on the more beautiful things in life – simple sunsets, sunrises, the breeze, or beautiful melodies coming from birds in the morning. When I'm with Mother Nature I feel blessed that I can see this beauty and feel it at the same time. All I need to do is close my eyes and listen, be in the moment.

In past times we were called witches, or sorcerers, or crazy women.
My personal belief is that schizophrenia can also be a gift, but a difficult one. Unfortunately, schizophrenics, I believe they have their doors wide open, and they have no idea how to close them. That's why they see so many things and hear so many horrible things.

I had a friend, Cathy. She was one of my lesbian friends. I

PART - FOUR Finishing up

mention this is because I was in a relationship with another woman (Joanna) who was Cathy's friend. Joanna was living in another city.

One day Cathy offered me a ride to pick up Joanna and bring her back to our city. The journey was long as she lived five hours away.

While we were driving, we had many conversations. One, was about an ex-girlfriend, Jenny. I knew Jenny has passed away, but I did not know when or why she died.

Cathy told me how much she missed Jenny and how much she loved her. When she was sharing her grief with me, she was emotional and had tears in her eyes.

At this very moment, whilst she was talking about Jenny, the spirit of Jenny appeared to me. I had no control over this as my breathing became heavy, almost like I could not catch my breath. I felt pressure on my chest. Then I saw her. She was standing in front of me, a bit to the left. She had beautiful wavy, brown hair past her shoulder and brown eyes. I let Cathy know that Jenny was there with us. She was uncertain and asked me to describe her, which I did. She gave a knowing but cautious nod. Cathy said, "Ask her if she has seen her brother?"

I did not need to ask Jenny the questions because Jenny could hear Cathy, but Cathy could not see or hear Jenny. I first asked her in my mind to please give me some sign that *you are real, and you are here with us*. Jenny could not look me in the eye. She looked sad, with her head down looking towards the ground where she was standing.
I replied to Cathy, "She's not answering".
Cathy asked, "Ask if she has seen her mother".
Once again Jenny did not answer. She just stood with her head bowed, looking miserable.
After a moment, Cathy said, "Ask her why she do it?"
Jenny finally answered. "I was tired...", then paused before continu-

ing to me, "She" (referring to Cathy), "does not believe that you are talking to me right now. Let it go, but if you want proof go to her apartment". Then Jenny slid away.

When we reached our destination, I was happy and excited to see Joanna. In private I told her what happened in the car with Cathy and Jenny. I told Joanna that when Cathy was telling me about Jenny, that's when Jenny came. She was able to come through me because I am 'an open person', with the gift. My doors are open and I know when and how to shut them.
Joanna explained to me that Cathy doesn't believe in such things. Yet, I know that Jenny used me as a vessel.

I also explained to Joanne that Jenny suggested I go to Cathy's place. I had never been there or had any idea what that was all about?
Joanna asked me not to talk about this anymore as Jenny committed suicide a year ago.

This explained why Jenny looked sad and would not answer the questions. It would seem she was stuck in limbo, not this side, not that side.

Anyway, we made our way back to Sydney. Our first stop was Cathy's place. As we walked into her apartment, in the hallway there was a picture frame with lots of little photos. Something compelled me to look at the photos. I saw that gorgeous face in one of the photos. It was Jenny. But in that photo, she had short hair. I stopped and I pointed the photo out to Joanna. That's the girl that I saw and spoke to when we were driving but she had long wavy hair.
Joanna replied, "Jenny had long hair before she cut it. Please leave it and do not speak about it again."

I understood why Jenny wanted me to go to Cathy's apartment. For my own peace of mind, she wanted me to see her picture as proof. I left it and never spoke of it again to either Joanna or Cathy.

My Angel

My Angel is still in my life, as my best friend. I dedicated this book to him as he has been there for me no matter what. For his kindness, his understanding, and never judging me. He is retired now and has two beautiful grandkids who he adores. From what I can see he is a wonderful grandfather. As I mentioned, he was also a kind of surrogate grandfather to my children when they were small – he changed plenty of nappies. He used to babysit them from time to time, helping to feed them and playing with them. So he had plenty of practice with babies. My girls, now as adults, know and admire this man.

I do not get to see him as often as before but we still keep in touch by phone. He is a blessing to me. I am glad I never met his wife as I could not look her straight into her eyes without feeling guilty. I do not want to be the woman known as her husband's lover.

Just in case you have wondered – I am not a man stealer. If I know the woman or if I have a female friend who is married, I would never go for her husband. Even if the husband tried to encourage me. If I know the woman or if she is a friend, I would not do that to her out of respect for her. However, if the man chooses to have an affair and I do not know the wife I do not see anything wrong with that. It is the man's thing because if it was not with me, it would be another woman – once a cheater, always a cheater. That is as long as I do not meet his wife.

Footnote. I write this (just before publishing), with a sad heart, and tears, My Angel has gone into dementia. I can now no longer communicate with him – I have tried. But his wife keeps taking the calls. She shouted that I was not to call, that she knows all about me, and that they nearly got divorced because of me. She asked me what I have to say for myself. I told her that she must ask him. As I write this, it is his birthday, and fuck it, I'm going to call him anyway... I want him to remember me and all the good that we had. I want to hear his voice. And that will be my closure in his part in my life.

Troy.
A scene from the movie Troy with Brad Pitt and Eric Bana. Conflict between two honourable and brave men who share the same beliefs – who must fight each other in honour of their kings.

Lee and Susanna

Happily, I have more than one angel in human form – my daughters. If it was not for them, I probably would not fight so hard to keep alcohol out of my life. They are my world, my inspiration, my

PART - FOUR Finishing up

anchor, and my reason to get up each day. I am close to my daughters and have a good relationship with them.

Since they were little I taught them to treat others as they would want to be treated. And, to be afraid of two things – mad people and guns because you never know when they're going to go off. I could joke and say, *I suppose that makes me mad*. Usually people that meet me say, "You're crazy…You're funny…" When my friends say this, it is a polite way of saying, "You're fucked in the head." Either way they mean well.

Unlike my upbringing, I always gave them lots of love, was there for them, listened to them, and most of all, did not judge or tell them they are stupid. And yes, I have fucked up in the past, I know I am not perfect. No one is. Like on that day when I was so drunk and fell asleep on the kitchen floor and they were under the table waiting for me to wake up. Whenever I think of this moment I feel pain, shame, and disgust. But I can't change that. I can only change what is now in front of me.

Lee is a young soul. She is a hard worker and determined to make something of her life in real estate. She works six days a week and she goes to TAFE at night to study. She will have her real estate license soon. I am so proud of her.

Susanna is spirited and as crazy as I am. Full of life and passion for others, kind hearted and speaks her mind. Let's hope she doesn't have to learn the hard way. She's a quick learner, street smart, and artistic. She does not yet recognise her drawing talent. I keep on telling her how good she is and with a bit of practice she could have a career as an artist. If she wishes to. She also has a beautiful voice. When she sings, I have goosebumps all over my body. I tell her, "You are sitting on a goldmine with that voice". But she says to me "I cannot sing on display". When she sings, it is with such passion and feeling. For example, when she sings Leonard Cohen's *And everybody knows* it comes out not just with her voice, but her face, her entire being – it is glorious.

4

Suzanne and I are close spiritually as she is an old soul. Each time I experience the other side, or when they haunt me, and they do, in my bedroom, if she is in her bedroom she will see and feel the same as I do. She'll dash into to my room and hide under the covers. After a while, when it settles, she'll snack in my bed as she tells me what she heard and saw. At the beginning I did not want to mess with her young head with such things. But how do you explain when two people in separate rooms see and hear the same stuff? It can't be in your head. This is for real. When she was young, I could not explain it properly, she was too young to understand. Now she's older I have explained that such a gift comes with consequences.
She is interested in doing psychology as she is very much intrigued by how the human mind works. Plus, she wants to help children with their struggles and addictions.

Their relationship with their father

Lee sees him a few times a month. But Susanna keeps away as he is too much of a bully. Don't get me wrong, they both love their father but he has mentally and emotionally abused her. She is a free spirit, but he is always trying to control how she dresses and what she thinks. Understandably, she doesn't want to see him as often.

Curiosity killed the cat

I had been a single mother since they were four and five years old, with no male figure living with us. When we used the toilet or bathroom, we never closed the door. This habit started when they were little and was safety based, so I could hear splashing and play-

PART - FOUR Finishing up

ing in the bath with toys. Knowing that they are okay in water.

Lee and Suzanne's primary school was in the next street and the girls were safe walking to and from school with other children and parents.
Usually, when they arrived from school, they would tell me about their day. But on this day, I was on the toilet. I had a period and so was wearing a period pad. The girls barged into the toilet and quickly noticed my pad, with a touch of blood. The questions quickly started;
Them; "Mummy what's that thing in your underpants?"
Me; "A nappy. This one is for mummies"
Them; "What is this on your nappy?"
Me; "Well you know how chickens have eggs?"
Them; "Yes".
Me; "Well we have eggs too. But you cannot see them as they are inside and so the blood pushes them out so new eggs can come and I can have a baby."
Them; "Mummy, can we have a baby?"
Me; "No. You need a special type of cuddle to have a baby."
Them; "But you cuddle us, so can we have a baby?!"
Me; "My darlings, the cuddle is a very special cuddle with a boy that you love."
Them; "Can you cuddle Daddy for a baby?" But Daddy doesn't live with us now so no cuddle from Daddy?"
Oh my God! question after question... I had to distract them so I asked them, "How was school?".

And that reminds me of another story. I give nicknames for their private parts, so when we go into a public toilet the other occupant cannot understand what we are talking about. For example, when we went to a public toilet I would say to Suzanne and Lee, " Make sure you wipe your cipcia (pussy in English) properly." And the boy's penis they called Dudu. They made that one up.

Arriving home one day they ran to me with excitement all over their face. "Mummy! Cipcia is called a vagina! And dudu is called a penis!"

Obviously they learned those words from school when they had an education about their own private parts.

I was shocked to hear my two little innocent girls use those words, penis and vagina. But on the other hand, I was happy they learned of these things at school and how to protect themselves.

My belief is that sex education should be more addressed in school, particularly high school. I know it's an embarrassing subject but they should understand that "yes" is yes, and "no" means no. Boys should have their own separate classroom when it comes to sex education, as should the girls. There would be less embarrassment and are likely to freely ask questions when they do not understand.

I look at the lack of my own sexual education from my family and school as a limitation for me at the time. This lack, as you have read, put me in many compromising situations. It should not be like that.

The first influence the child picks up is from their parents. When in primary school they can pick up wrong habits just to fit in. Or they hide within and become bookworms – there is nothing wrong with that.

If you are a teacher reading this, do something about it. Sex education should be introduced in high school. Better understanding would reduce coercion and rape. Children would learn self-respect for their own bodies. And I am sure that the bullying that goes on in school would reduce as well.

Dreams

I don't like reading. How funny, here I am writing this book. It

PART - FOUR Finishing up

has been written in a simple way, so everyone will be able to read it. There is nothing worse than reading a book and it doesn't make sense or you do not understand it because it's hard to read.

When I was a teenager, I wanted to be a model. A supermodel. I wanted to be well-known and rich. Have fortune and fame. Now I am older, I do not desire these things. What I enjoy the most is peace and quiet. I love meditation and listening to the birds early in the morning or listening to my favourite music. It might sound simplistic but doing those simple things brings me peace of mind – like I've been hypnotized. No one to disturb the quiet, just the beautiful melody and the sound of the birds. And with the early-morning sun, I close my eyes and lift my face towards the sun to feel its warmth. I adore my art, and of course, being with my daughters. When doing these things, I forget all my worries at that moment.

I have shared a few of my secrets with you. I have, of course, changed the names of the characters and over-dramatised some of the stories for a more interesting read (I call this a good imagination). But I do not remember my childhood very clearly. What I have shared with you are some of the moments that stand out. To be honest, I do not want to remember my childhood as I don't have very many happy memories. For example, me being molested by my grandfather and others. I try to block those memories. Writing this book was very hard, reliving those moments. But this book, and my paintings, is my dedication and legacy for my children.

And I am hoping to inspire whoever reads this book; do not stop believing in yourself. Whatever you want to achieve in your life, write it down on a piece of paper. Take it to one of your favourite pot plants. Fold the paper and dig it into the dirt. Leave the pot plant outside on a balcony or in your garden. Let nature take its course. Don't forget to work towards your desire. There, I just gave you a spell for your success, see I must be a witch. Try it, it's not gonna hurt you. You've got nothing to lose. But remember, be true to your heart and whatever you write on a piece of paper you must hold good intent and positive thinking.

I am writing this book during the Covid19 pandemic, and Sydney's long lockdown. I hope that all of us do the right thing for each other. I pray each day for my family and those who are lost. And if you find yourself reading this book, remember that you are not alone. Just trust yourself and your gut instinct for what you want to achieve in your life. All I want is peace and quiet. No more wars, no more violence. Just love! Is that too much to ask? We can all start by being nice to one another. Smile at the stranger and say hello. That reminds me of the time when one day I went into the city, my last story for you.

After parking my car in the parking lot, I went off. On my way I walked by a homeless person. He was dirty, hungry, and cold. He asked me for some money. I gave him what I had left without thinking that I needed it for the parking station. When I returned to the car park, and in the queue to pay, it was then I realised I did not have any money. I tried to explain this to the man in the cash booth, that I gave my last coins to a homeless person.

Suddenly, I felt a tap on my shoulder. When I turned around the man behind me offered money to pay for my car spot. I did not expect that, but you see what I mean by Guardian Angels. You never know who is watching your back.

Second chance

Life is beautiful, in as much as there are always opportunities to see the light, to get off the street, to clean up your act, for others to show kindness. I started my life in hell and remained there for many years. But life offered me another chance (it always does).

PART - FOUR Finishing up

It was up to me, in my hands. I wrote this book for the many out there, who like me, have no control over their destiny. There is hope, you are lovable – work hard and you will find it.

Goodbye, I hope I can entertain you again soon.

If you would like to see my art, please visit my website

www.AnnaMariaartist.com

Love to you all!

www.ingramcontent.com/pod-product-compliance
Lightning Source LLC
Chambersburg PA
CBHW052145070526
44585CB00017B/1986